Using Storytelling to Support Children and Adults with Special Needs

This innovative and wide-ranging book shows how storytelling can open new worlds for learners with or without special educational needs.

Outlining both therapeutic and educational approaches, the leading practitioners who contribute to this practical resource draw upon their extensive experience to provide inspiration for your own lessons. Providing a highly accessible combination of theory and practice, the contributors to this book:

- Define their own approach to storytelling
- Describe the principles and theory that underpin their practice
- Demonstrate how they work with different types of story
- Provide extensive case-studies and assessment frameworks for a range of different special needs and age ranges
- Provide some 'top tips' for practitioners who want to start using stories in this way

Using Storytelling to Support Children and Adults with Special Needs will be of interest to all education professionals as well as therapists, youth workers, counsellors, and storytellers and theatre practitioners working in special education.

Nicola Grove is the founder of Openstorytellers, the first arts company of intellectually disabled storytellers (www.openstorytellers.org.uk). She is Honorary Research Fellow in the Department of Language and Communication Science at City University London, UK. She has published widely in the field of special needs and communication.

Using Storytelling to Support Children and Adults with Special Needs

Transforming lives through telling tales

Edited by Nicola Grove

Routledge
Taylor & Francis Group

LONDON AND NEW YORK

First published 2013
by Routledge
2 Park Square, Milton Park, Abingdon, Oxon OX14 4RN

Simultaneously published in the USA and Canada
by Routledge
711 Third Avenue, New York, NY 10017

Routledge is an imprint of the Taylor & Francis Group, an informa business

British Library Cataloguing in Publication Data
A catalogue record for this book is available from the British Library

Library of Congress Cataloging in Publication Data
A catalog record for this book has been requested

ISBN: 978-0-415-68775-1 (pbk)
ISBN: 978-0-203-08092-4 (ebk)

Typeset in Galliard
by Swales & Willis Ltd, Exeter

MIX
Paper from
responsible sources
FSC
www.fsc.org   FSC® C004839

Printed and bound in Great Britain by the MPG Books Group

Contents

Notes on contributors

Rolf Black has been working with children with complex disabilities since 1993. Being a mechanical engineer and bioengineer, his work first focused on walking orthoses for children with spina bifida and cerebral palsy. He developed a mechanism for an orthotic hip joint and co-founded EO-Funktion (now Made for Movement) in Germany to directly supply a special dynamic walking frame to children with severe motor disabilities, many of whom had no or little functional speech. This experience led in 2005 to Rolf joining Annalu Waller and her team at the University of Dundee as a researcher in alternative and augmentative communication. His main interests are personal narrative and literacy for children with complex communication needs. He has co-initiated research projects such as 'The PhonicStick' and 'How was School today . . .?', the latter winning the TES Outstanding ICT Learning Initiative of the Year award in 2010 for its participating school.

Louise Coigley is an independent speech and language therapist and a trained storyteller (School of Storytelling and Artemis School of Speech and Drama) and curative educator (Camphill). She works at a school for children with emotional and behavioural problems. Lis'n Tell: Live Inclusive Storytelling is an approach Louise has developed over 28 years. She teaches Lis'n Tell on speech and language therapy training courses, nationally and internationally, to parents, therapists and teachers (www.lisntell.com).

Janet Dowling is a storyteller who specialises in telling stories and working with metaphor to inspire and to make a difference. Drawing on her previous work and experience as a psychiatric social worker, she develops stories with children, families, adults and communities to find their own storytelling voice, celebrating their unity, community and diversity. She is a Winston Churchill Memorial Trust Fellow for storytelling in bereavement and uses storytelling as part of her work as a Cruse Bereavement Care volunteer. She worked for 3 years as a therapeutic storyteller at the Children's Trust in Tadworth, Surrey with children recovering from acquired brain injury or with profound, multiple learning disabilities.

Barbara Fornefeld studied special education with an emphasis on the education of people with mental disabilities. After working as a special teacher and university lecturer, she received her doctorate in 1989 on the concept of 'Elementary Relationship'. Since 1990 she has been working as a professor at the universities of Ludwigsburg/Reutlingen, Heidelberg and Cologne. Her field of research is the education and rehabilitation of people with profound intellectual and multiple disabilities (PIMD) within national and international contexts. In 1994 she completed a postdoctoral qualification at the

University of Cologne on the theory of the special education of people with profound disabilities. Currently, her research interest is focused on the development of cultural possibilities for people with PIMD.

Chris Fuller has taught in both mainstream and special schools. In the 1980s she wrote and designed the prototypes for six multisensory story-packs to enable children with profound intellectual and multiple disabilities in her school to access and enjoy stories. In 1989 her 'do-it-yourself' manual was published, but later research indicated that many readers lacked the time to assemble the stories. She then secured National Lottery funding to found and head Bag Books, a company with charitable status employing skilled craft artists to produce story-packs. Multisensory storytelling and training tours throughout the UK followed, and within 15 years the number of titles grew to 37. Bag Books has now produced and distributed over ten thousand story-packs. Now retired, Chris is a member of the editorial group for the journal *PMLDLINK* and is on the board of trustees for ClearVision, a postal library for children with visual impairment.

Carol Gray is President of The Gray Center for Social Learning and Understanding in Zeeland, Michigan, a non-profit organisation serving people with autism spectrum disorders (ASD) and those working on their behalf. She is an internationally respected author and speaker with 30 years' experience as a teacher and consultant working on behalf of children and adults with ASD. In 1991, Carol developed Social Stories™, a strategy used worldwide with children with ASD. She has published several articles, chapters and books addressing such challenging issues as how to teach social understanding and social skills; bullying; death and dying; loss and learning; and categorisation and generalisation. Carol is the recipient of several awards for her international contribution to the education and welfare of people with ASD.

Nicola Grove PhD started out as an English teacher and turned into a speech and language therapist 35 years ago, specialising in the use of sign language, early communication and the design of inclusive programmes of study for the National Curriculum. She developed resources to support access to literature for all pupils, and then discovered traditional storytelling. Since 2004 she has been practising as a storyteller and facilitator of storymaking with children and adults who have communication and learning difficulties. She set up Openstorytellers, a charity which empowers people at risk of social exclusion through the use of narrative (www.openstorytellers.org.uk). She runs projects and training courses in schools, day centres and residential homes. She is exploring constructs of learning difficulties in myths and legends, visiting South Africa, Japan, Australia and Canada in search of stories that can empower tellers and listeners, and challenge social exclusion.

Jane Harwood is a workshop leader, storyteller, musician and music leader working in and outside educational settings. Her experience of teaching all ages and abilities includes much work with learning-disabled adults and children. She has worked with the charity Openstorytellers since its inception. She also runs two small organisations, Count Me In (community music) and Strata Collective (media arts/landscape). Jane runs Storysharing groups with adults and children, including many with profound and multiple disabilities and sensory impairments. She is currently engaged in delivering a 3-year action-based research project that investigates the impact of shared personal narratives on the lives of young people with complex communication needs.

James Hogg has undertaken research in the field of profound and multiple disabilities (PIMD) for a number of years, and through the White Top Research Unit at the University of Dundee works closely with *PAMIS* on research into and evaluation of the organisation's activities. Over the past 5 years he has undertaken research into adult safeguarding for the Scottish government, participating in the local and national implementation of adult support and protection legislation.

Sue Jennings PhD is an author, storyteller, play and dramatherapist who works internationally as a trainer and project leader. She started life as a professional dancer and actor before devoting her middle years to the pioneering of drama and theatre as therapy. Her doctoral research was with the Temiar of the Malaysian rain forest, where storytelling has a central role in community cohesiveness. Most of her time is now divided between the UK and Romania, where she lives and writes both stories and therapy books.

Victoria Joffe PhD is a specialist speech and language therapist and senior lecturer in developmental speech, language and communication impairments in the Department of Language and Communication Science at City University, London. Victoria runs various workshops for trusts, local authorities and schools on child speech disorder, evidence-based practice in speech and language therapy and collaborative practice in education, and provides training for therapists and teaching staff on working with children and young adults with speech, language and communication needs in education. Victoria is currently involved in a large-scale intervention project, funded by the Nuffield Foundation, on enhancing language and communication in secondary school children with language impairments, on which this programme is based.

Loretto Lambe founded *PAMIS*, University of Dundee, 20 years ago, developing support services for families caring for a member with PIMD throughout Scotland. As director of the organisation she undertakes innovative research into a wide range of issues of concern to such families, notably on healthy lifestyles and leisure and, more recently, self-directed support. With colleagues she has developed the concepts and practice of multisensory storytelling and is at present undertaking a study of bereavement and PIMD. She ensures that issues to do with people with PIMD are carried into national and international forums of which she is a member, notably the Royal Society of Medicine Forum on Intellectual Disability and the International Association for the Scientific Study of Intellectual Disability Special Interest Research Group on PIMD.

Beth McCaffrey PhD completed a MEd in 1996 (*Can the Excluded Become Included?*), using story to develop empathy in 6 to 7-year-olds, and went on to complete her doctoral dissertation at the University of Exeter in 2009. She has been teaching for 15 years at a special school for pupils with moderate learning difficulties and other complex needs.

Keith Park has worked in a number of educational settings in the UK and Australia for more years than he cares to remember. With Nicola Grove he is the co-author of *Odyssey Now*, the first book to make classical literature accessible to people with severe and profound learning disabilities. Keith is a teacher, writer and performer and runs inclusive workshops on a variety of topics and in a variety of community settings, including Shakespeare at the Globe Theatre, Bible stories in cockney rhyming slang at Westminster Abbey, and Hans Christian Andersen at the Royal Academy of Arts.

Tuula Pulli PhD is a Finnish adventurer on leave, still seeking treasures with her grandson. As a speech therapist she specialises in hearing, autism, language and developmental disorders. She has researched, lectured and published about alternative and augmentative communication (AAC), community-based rehabilitation, creative and trans-disciplinary teamwork and drama education, with many publications in Finnish and Swedish, and some conference abstracts in English. She is Finland's representative for a long-term network developing AAC with persons with profound learning disability in northern countries, and she has also worked in China. In the 1990s she started a study of drama with communities and staff working with persons with multiple disabilities who cannot speak, gaining her doctorate in 2010. Now retired, she is lightening the darkness by developing and researching applied and devised drama and storytelling, and listening to messages from the archives of literature and hermeneutic philosophy.

Becky Shanks works as a senior specialist speech and language therapist in North Wales for Betsi Cadwaladr University local health board as part of the speech and language therapy mainstream school team. She has worked collaboratively with education for more than 15 years in both England and Wales, promoting integrated speech and language therapy services to children and young people within primary and secondary mainstream settings. She developed the *Speaking and Listening Through Narrative* approach in 2001 as part of a collaborative project with education whilst working in Stockport. She continues to work with Black Sheep Press to develop and extend a range of resources based on her approach for children and young people in both primary and secondary settings.

Ingeborg Sungen studied English with an emphasis on American literature and French at Duisburg University, Germany. Since 1982 she has been working for film festivals in Oberhausen and Mannheim and for the Theatre for Young People in Dortmund, and she also works for film and television in national and international productions. She has been editing and translating for 30 years and is currently working as a secretary at Cologne University.

Annalu Waller PhD holds a personal chair in Human Communication Technologies in the School of Computing at the University of Dundee. She has worked in the field of augmentative and alternate communication (AAC) since 1985, designing communication systems for and with non-speaking individuals. She established the first AAC assessment and training centre in South Africa in 1987. Her primary research areas are human computer interaction, natural language processing, personal narrative and assistive technology. In particular, she focuses on empowering end-users, including disabled adults and children, by involving them in the design and use of technology. She manages a number of interdisciplinary research projects with industry and practitioners from rehabilitation engineering, special education, speech and language therapy, nursing and dentistry. She is on the editorial boards of several academic journals and sits on the boards of a number of national and international organisations representing disabled people.

Introduction

Nicola Grove

> The creation myth is the story that enacts the creative power of stories, the many narratives that are going on in us all the time, and in which we live. Scheherazade, herself a story, tells tales to you non-stop to keep you awake, and thereby saves your life as well as her own.
>
> (Don Cupitt, 1991)

Telling stories is one of the simplest, most enjoyable and most transformative activities on earth. With this book we hope to inspire everyone who is interested in the lives of children and adults with special needs and disabilities – in homes, classrooms, arts facilities, social services and health services – to feel that they can tell stories in ways that are fun, creative and empowering.

Recent years have seen a surge of interest in the power of oral storytelling in both therapeutic and educational contexts. There is now general recognition that many children come into school with limited language skills, and leave with poor levels of literacy and oracy, which will affect their life chances. Oral storytelling has been shown to develop language comprehension, emotional well-being, empathy, a sense of identity, imagination, creativity and literacy skills (see, for example, Curenton et al., 2008; Haven, 2007; Snow et al., 1998; Griffin et al., 2004; Reese et al., 2010; Reese et al., 2010; Van Puyenbroeck & Maes, 2008). The field of special needs in particular has seen a number of exciting storytelling approaches that have transformed the learning experience of children and adults with a wide range of difficulties. The many approaches on offer are exciting, but also challenging. What kind of storytelling do you want? How do you know what will best suit your students? How does a particular approach fit with your working priorities – and indeed your own interests and skills?

About this book

The book grew from a short survey I conducted in 2009 with colleagues who were using story in different ways in different settings. I heard from those who had been working for many years, but I also became aware of some very innovative new projects which would inevitably take some time to write up and publish. However, in my many visits to schools and centres, I found that professionals were often only aware of one or two ways of telling stories. The time seemed ripe to suggest an overview of some of the tried and tested, as well as the new approaches on offer.

Many years ago, when I was beginning to explore the potential of stories and storytelling, a colleague suggested I read Michael Bamberg's book *Narrative Development: Six Approaches*[1]. Taking its title from Wallace Steven's famous poem, 'Thirteen Ways of Looking at a Blackbird', which itself drew on William Empson's essay, 'Seven Types of Ambiguity', this is a collection which facilitates the study of complex perspectives on narrative by addressing the same set of questions in each chapter. It suggests that there is no one approach which is superior to any other, but that the framework which is adopted to defining and implementing narrative will influence the questions that you ask and the answers you can provide.

We want readers to understand what the different approaches involve, and the history, theory and principles that guided their development. Next, we want to illustrate how the approach may work in practice, to know what the outcomes are likely to be, and to have access to relevant evidence. As not all approaches will necessarily work with every single student, we have pointed out issues to consider and possible limitations. Cultural considerations are important in all interventions, and storytelling is no exception. Finally, we want readers to feel inspired to go and try things out for themselves, to have practical tips to bear in mind, and to know where to go for training.

You should therefore find the following issues discussed in each chapter, bearing in mind that authors have addressed the task at different levels of detail and in different ways, appropriate to their philosophy and implementation frameworks. However, the final two chapters have different emphases – on guidelines for the use of narrative with communication aids, and on evaluative frameworks.

- **Background**
  - A description of the particular approach and a definition of the terms 'story' and 'narrative'.
    The principles and theory that underpin the practice.
  - Relevant history, sometimes very personal, of how the approach was developed.
- **Work in practice**
  - A description of a typical session.
  - The use of different kinds of stories – fictional, personal, traditional or a combination.
  - How the work is evaluated – outcomes, any assessments used, what the practitioner looks for to determine whether the child is learning, progressing or simply enjoying and engaging.
  - An illustration or two of how an individual or group responded to the approach. *All the names used here are pseudonyms unless otherwise indicated.*
- **Issues to consider**
  - Any limitations or problems that come up, with suggestions for tackling them.
  - Any groups who need special consideration.
  - Cultural questions that affect the involvement of people from other communities.
- **Try it yourself**
  - Top three tips for practitioners who want to start using stories in their work.
  - Where to go – further information and resources.

Why now?

There are many reasons why this book is timely. Children and professionals are facing huge challenges; many are entering school with poor language and communication skills. In the

UK approximately 20% of the school population at any one time are said to have special educational needs (SENs). Between the ages of 5 and 7 years around half of these needs are identified as speech and language difficulties. These problems may have a knock-on effect; as pupils get older, the main difficulties reported are to do with literacy, and then by ages of 12–17 years, behavioural difficulties (Bercow, 2008). The same report demonstrates that children with special educational needs are severely underachieving and are disadvantaged when leaving school and making choices of further study or a career. Cuts to speech and language therapy services, and a planned reduction in statements of special educational needs, mean that teachers are going to have to manage even more challenges in the classroom with little external support. Storytelling is a powerful practical activity: a proven method of engaging children that everyone can join in.

What is storytelling?

Because storytelling is such a diverse practice, there are many different ideas and perceptions of what it involves. All oral tellers are used to having to correct misunderstandings about the nature of their work: 'no, we don't read stories we tell them', 'no, it's not just for children', 'no, we aren't creative writers as such' (though an orally told story can lead to literacy). Fundamentally, storytelling is an oral art, involving the transmission of tales that have been handed down 'from mouth to ear',[2] sometimes mediated by written forms. If you are deaf, the stories will have been (literally) handed down manually between hand and eye through sign language. Deaf people are amazing storytellers, as anyone who has been privileged to sit amongst a gathering of signing friends will tell you. The focus of this book is the live interactive construction of stories, rather than the creation of stories as output (written or digitised), although this may indeed be an important goal or tool in the process (Sutton-Spence 2010).

Why storytelling?

This ancient creative art form has been used in all societies to entertain, record events and instruct. As the Story Museum in Oxford[3] puts it, storytelling involves direct, immediate, face-to-face interactions that engage attention amd require active listening and inter-pretation. Through stories we find out about new experiences and ideas, we develop empathy and imagination, and we learn how to face challenges and solve problems. Good narrative abilities seem to be associated with literacy and general educational achievement, probably because telling stories to others involves the manipulation of complex language, cognitive and social processes – talking about events removed from the here and now, sequencing, creating causal and temporal links, and simultaneously holding the attention of the listener (Melzi & Caspe, 2008; Reese et al., 2010).

However, in educational settings, the oral component of story has been minimised. In the UK National Curriculum, speaking and listening has been subordinated to literacy for the last 20 years (it is literacy that is tested, not oracy). Although there are a few mentions within the speaking and listening strand of English, virtually everything relating to story and narrative is subsumed within literacy, and its subdivision, literature, with some use in drama. It is perhaps because of this that teachers get confused. Some years ago I contributed a section to a training manual for newly qualified teachers about oral narrative tasks for young people with special needs. I gave some training to a group, based on the chapter. Some months later I was asked if I would go back and support some of the teachers concerned because they were finding it difficult to implement. I asked what the difficulties were. 'Oh,' said one young woman, 'I tried doing what you suggested but it just didn't work.' I enquired further: who were her students? They turned out to be teenage boys with emotional and behavioural difficulties. What was the problem? 'Well,' she said, 'they are just really scared of reading and writing.' Maybe I had not been clear enough in my original lecture, but the chapter she was working from specifically stated that this was an oral approach! These attitudes are persistent and pervasive: in a recent radio interview about the need to train childminders, literacy and reading was emphasised, not conversation or storytelling.[4]

Special educational needs and disabilities

What do we mean by special needs? The term is used within the education sector in the UK, and is defined as needs that affect a child's ability to learn and function well in the school community: cognitive and learning needs; language and communication needs; social and emotional needs; sensory needs (visual and hearing impairments) and physical needs. Some are temporary; for example, a pupil may have specific emotional needs in response to a crisis, or physical difficulties resulting from an illness, which subsequently resolve. Other needs will be pervasive and result in people identifying themselves, or being identified by others, as having disabilities in adult life.

Many of the contributors to this book work with adults as well as children. The approaches have been developed with: children and adults with moderate, severe and profound intellectual or learning disabilities[5]; children with developmental language delay, acquired brain injury or autistic spectrum difficulties; and those who suffer emotional deprivation. The needs which result are related to cognitive, language, emotional, creative, social, physical and spiritual development. For example, although we do not directly address the issue of hearing impairment and deafness, all practitioners recommend using sign and multisensory approaches.

Terminology

Storytelling is proving so popular that we practitioners are struggling somewhat to define approaches in ways that are precise and indicative. You will find that most authors here identify a multisensory dimension to their work: what we might call generic (small 'm') multisensory. Lambe and Hogg (see Chapter 11) and colleagues in Europe use the term Multisensory Storytelling – MSST ('big M') as their trade name. Similarly, all oral storytelling is interactive (small 'i') but Keith Park (see Chapter 5) coined the term Interactive Storytelling (big 'I') for his call and response approach, because this is the element that he felt was most distinctive in his work. In this volume we have tried to recognise the commonalities between approaches as well as respecting professional boundaries.

Reading, telling, performing

Because of the long association between books and stories, the term 'storytelling' tends to be used to cover reading as well as oral telling. At the other end of the continuum there is a close relationship between telling, as narration, and performing, as dramatisation. At the extremes there are clear distinctions (e.g. in drama, characters engage in dialogue in real time, whereas in narrative, speech is reported). But one of the joys of using story is that it is possible to move between different modes. Thus McCaffrey starts by reading, moves into drama, and then towards telling and writing. Three authors (Fuller, Lambe and Fornefeld) locate their work firmly within the tradition of reading stories out loud. They use prewritten scripts in order to ensure consistency of delivery and opportunities for repeated learning, as does Gray with her social stories. Other authors (Dowling, Jennings, Grove and Harwood, Coigley, Pulli) operate more spontaneously, in accordance with a fundamental principle of oral storytelling, which is that each story is told anew because the teller is responsive to the particular audience. However, the anecdotes developed by Grove and Harwood do eventually become scripted through repeated telling and practice. And Park, whose call and response approach is highly oral, keeps to a script every bit as strictly as Fuller, Lambe and Hogg, because of the importance of the metrical beat.

Types of story

Most authors are working with many different types of story: traditional (myths, legends, wonder tales and fables), fictional (i.e. authored), personal experiences, and stories that the teller, or the child, makes up for themselves to suit the occasion. Some authors use predominantly one type. Thus Fornefeld explicitly uses fairy tales and biblical stories (but also invents stories); Lambe and Hogg, Gray, Grove and Harwood describe personal anecdotes and stories of life events; Fuller has crafted her own stories and designed packs for other authors' stories. One issue is that genre type does influence the ease with which children master narrative structure. Everyday accounts (such as those involved in Social Stories™) and personal narratives pose less of a challenge than retold fictional stories or generated stories, both for typically developing children (Allen et al., 1994; Hudson & Shapiro, 1991) and those with language impairments (McCabe et al., 2008). However, as Waller and Black suggest in their chapter on narratives by children using aided communication, in some circumstances it may be that fictional narratives are easier than personal event recounts – when they are known and predictable, and offer structured opportunities for participation. In children's development, it is clear that there is an interaction between types of narrative; as children become more exposed to literate fictional stories, there is feedback into their own narrative constructions (Fox, 1993). We need to nurture all types of stories and storytelling, and it is clear from these chapters that individuals thrive when the storyteller is able to tailor the selection of the stories to their particular circumstances and interests.

Telling to, telling with, telling by

Most of the chapters cover strategies for telling *to* children and adults with disabilities but they all insist on active participation *by* individuals in the process. Some (Shanks, Joffe, Grove, Grove and Harwood, Waller and Black) have a more explicit focus on the development of narrative skills, moving towards independent narration from a supportive position – telling *with* individuals. In all cases, the concern is to develop the potential of the children and adults who are involved in the storytelling. The main dimensions of learning and development are *emotional and social* (what might be termed therapeutic or relational); *cognitive and linguistic* (educational); *creative* (arts practice); *community participation*; *leisure/enjoyment* and, finally, *emancipator and political*. In some approaches there is one particular focus; in others the purposes are intertwined and inseparable.

Narrative and story

Each author was invited to provide a definition of the broad category of narrative and the narrower category of story – and many have done so. In all cases, narrative is defined as the conveying of a sequence of events that are linked in time (*temporality*) and by consequence (*causality*). One event, as we say, leads to another. Story, however, is another matter, and the way that authors chose to define this was governed by their own perspective. These definitions offer options to the reader; if you want to emphasise a particular aspect of story then look for a definition that meets this situation. For example, Shanks (see Chapter 6) places the focus on cognitive and language skills, whereas Park (see Chapter 5) focuses on the poetic, and Pulli (see Chapter 15) focuses on social and aesthetic elements. Gray sees her social stories as more like narratives, as the entertainment aspect is not prominent. However, what Social Stories™ demonstrate very clearly is the ancient educational role of storytelling in illustrating how we should conduct ourselves in our relations with others and in different situations. Of course, you do not have to be restricted by any one definition: McCaffrey (see Chapter 3) used a multidimensional framework for her research.

Cultural issues

In the world of oral storytelling, cultural styles and cultural ownership are hotly disputed topics. How we can authentically tell stories from other traditions than our own poses real ethical problems. Many of the tales that are circulating readily in published books were taken down by (largely white, Western) anthropologists, tidied up and divorced from their original sacred or ritual contexts.

> Within our culture there's a number of categories of stories: public stories, sacred stories, sacred secret stories, men's and women's stories. A woman cannot tell a man's story to a group of men and men cannot tell women's stories – I don't know the men's stories – I only know the female, the public, the women's and sacred stories – stories just for women.
>
> (Pauline McLeod, Aboriginal Storyteller,
> interviewed in 1998 by Helen McKay for *Telling Tales*[6])

Eric Maddern, an experienced storyteller and traveller, puts the challenge head on:

> By what right do storytellers tell stories from Africa, Native America, Aboriginal Australia and other similar cultures? Isn't appropriating and telling these peoples' stories an extension of colonialism? We stole their lands and livelihoods; we decimated their cultures; we virtually drove them to extinction. Now we want to tell their stories. Isn't this just the latest stage of colonial theft? It's not surprising that some survivors from such cultures think so.[7]

So we need to be culturally sensitive in choosing the stories we tell to people (see Keith Park's chapter for ways of collaborating with those who own the stories). We also need to be sensitive to cultural differences as we seek to develop oral skills of telling, which can differ considerably between different ethnic traditions and language backgrounds, and within different genres of story. Comparative research from the USA demonstrates the serious consequences when there is too much of a mismatch between the expectations of teachers

and the experiences of pupils (Dickinson, 1991; Heath, 1982; Michaels, 1981). For example, Vernon Feagans and co-researchers (2002) showed that despite having superior skills in
vocabulary and narrative, the storytelling abilities of African American boys from low income
families were *negatively* associated with literacy and educational outcomes, probably because
their elaborated, sophisticated retellings did not conform to the simple and straightforward
paraphrases that their teachers required. Grove and Harwood, Chapter 13, provide a brief
discussion of cultural issues in personal storytelling, based on work by McCabe and Bliss
(2003). Many contributors have used their approaches successfully with children and adults
from a wide range of cultural backgrounds, but there still remains a great deal to research
and learn about indigenous traditions and what they can teach us.[8]

About the authors

The contributors to this book are all highly creative practitioners in the art of story, whether
myths and legends, written literature, personal stories, life stories and biography, or stories
created by children themselves. The purposes and methods are diverse. Therapeutic,
educational and leisure aims can be identified; usually we are looking at a happy mixture
of all three. Different models and frameworks are used in the design and to guide what
practitioners seek to achieve (assessments, evaluations and progression frameworks). Some
authors have been in a position to undertake rigorous research – reported here. The evidence
from others is based more on their long experience, observations and reports from colleagues
and the many children, adults, families and professionals who have benefited from their work.

Reading this book

The first chapters are those which come from a specifically therapeutic perspective. Janet
Dowling, a counsellor, and Sue Jennings, a play and drama therapist, describe the ways they
have worked with children facing emotional crises caused by illness and injury, and by neglect
and abuse. This sets the tone – the provision of a healing, regenerative space is one of the
most important gifts we can offer through story, even if we are not specifically trained in
therapeutic methods, as Beth McCaffrey demonstrates in her account of a successful and
creative storytelling project in a special needs classroom. Beth's work involves a complex
mixture of literacy, oracy and drama. Louise Coigley shares with Keith Park an emphasis on
drama, ritual and repetition (as does Tuula Pulli's work described in the final chapter). The
next three chapters all focus on the explicit teaching of narrative skills: Becky Shanks' work,
and that of her colleague Judith Carey, has long been influential in the nursery and primary
sector, and has recently been extended to an upper age of 14 years. Both she and Victoria
Joffe, whose recent successful programme targets secondary aged pupils and young adults,
focus on strategies for helping pupils master the structural elements of storytelling, using
visual prompts and carefully prepared questions. The chapter which follows, 'Learning to
Tell', describes an approach aimed at young people and adults to enable them to develop
skills as community storytellers – building up a repertoire of tales, linking these to personal
experience and developing collaborative telling styles.

The succeeding chapters have a focus on multisensory storytelling with children and adults
who have severe and profound learning disabilities. Fornefeld and colleagues work to provide
resources for sharing culturally important stories using delightful and beautifully crafted
artefacts. Fuller developed multi-sensory stories in story-packs some 20 years ago when she
was teaching in a special school; these have become a landmark in inclusive literacy, and have

been developed by Lambe and Hogg and colleagues in Europe in many innovative ways: here we focus on the work of *PAMIS* in producing resources around sensitive issues such as sexuality, health and bereavement. Grove and Harwood also work with personal narratives: Storysharing™ is a technique based on conversational anecdotal telling which is also applicable to fictional and traditional stories, and which has proved very accessible to individuals who are not able to tell stories independently, including those with severe autism.

The theme of everyday stories continues with Carol Gray's widely used work on 'social' stories. This has been shown to support people who find it hard to understand and adapt their behaviour to social situations, transitions and unexpected events. Research by Schank and Abelson (1977), and St Clair and Busch (2003) on social scripts, and Nelson (Nelson, 1999; Nelson & Gruendel, 1986) on generalised event representations, support Gray's insights into what she terms 'small unassuming stories of everyday life' in helping individuals to understand and make inferences about what will happen in social situations. Nelson's work also shows the crucial role of general knowledge about events in the development of autobiographic memory general events (Nelson, 1999; Nelson & Gruendel, 1986). Common to all personal storytelling is the necessity for careful preparation and adaptation to individuals so that each story is uniquely owned and told, with an absolute commitment to respecting and valuing the children and adults who are worked with.

Waller and Black's chapter summarises the work they have done over many years with children and young adults who use augmentative and alternative communication, highlighting the very particular challenges that they face in telling their own stories spontaneously. Finally, Tuula Pulli describes the evaluative framework that she developed to explore in-depth the complex creative interactions that lie at the heart of the storytelling experience.

What else?

The focus of this book is on the process of live, dynamic, face-to-face storytelling. Two areas that are not covered here are life story work with adults, and the new and expanding field of digital storytelling. Life-history work (Atkinson et al., 2010) is a distinct discipline within disability studies which is assuming increasing importance as people start to take control of their own lives and their own biographies; however, the emphasis until very recently has been on the testimonies themselves as transcribed texts, rather than on the process of oral transmission, which placed it somewhat outside the boundaries of this volume. Another related area is digital storytelling, which has been revolutionised by the impact of new devices that at the time the book was conceived were not even in production. It is certain that the world of oral telling will be transformed once practitioners, families and people with disabilities themselves get familiar with interactive mobile technology that will allow them to upload pictures, films and three-dimensional images of objects to integrate into their storytelling and story conversations. A brief review can be found in Appendix 2. For now we can only say that this book could have become a never-ending story, such is the reach of narrative into our lives.

And we all lived . . .

In conclusion, we all hope that this book will prove a resource for readers to develop their own creative practice. There are as many stories as there are stars in the sky – and as many ways of telling.

There is a Seneca legend about how stories came into the world.[9] A magic story rock tells tales to a whole community who come to listen, but then commands the people to go out and tell for themselves. In the words of Brian Marshall, a founder member of Openstorytellers, who has Down's syndrome: 'We all have stories, don't we?' But many people lack a voice to tell, so let's enable everyone to be heard and everyone to enjoy the power of story.

Notes

1   Thanks to Professor John Clibbens, University of Essex, for this recommendation.
2   www.sfs.org.uk.
3   www.storymuseum.org.uk.
4   BBC Radio 4 Today Programme, 23 March 2012. Interview with Ann Longfield, Director of 4Children.
5   In the UK the term learning disabilities denotes intellectual disabilities, whereas in the USA learning disabilities denotes educational difficulties, such as with reading, writing or number.
6   www.australianstorytelling.org.au/txt/mcleod.php [retrieved 24 February 2012].
7   http://matthewfinch.me/2011/04/16/telling-stories-from-cultures-not-our-own/ [retrieved 24 February 2012].
8   www.marilynkinsella.org [retrieved 13April 2012]. Advice on telling stories from different cultures.
9   http://www.firstpeople.us/FP-Html-Legends/The-Origin-Of-Stories-Seneca.html   [retrieved 13 April 2012].

References

Allen, M., Kertoy, M., Sherblom, J. & Pettit, J. (1994). Children's narrative productions: A comparison of personal event and fictional stories. *Applied Psycholinguistics, 15,* 149–176.

Atkinson, D., Holland, C., Humber, L., Ingham, N., Ledger, S. & Tilley, E. (2010). *Developing a 'living archive' of learning disability life stories: Project report.* Milton Keynes: Open University Press.

Bercow, J. (2008). *The Bercow report: A review of services for children and young people (0–19) with speech, language and communication needs.* Available at: https://www.education.gov.uk/publications/standard/publicationDetail/Page1/DCSF-00632-2008.

Cupitt, D. (1991). *What is a story?* Norwich: SCM Press.

Curenton, S., Jones Craig, M. & Flanagan, N. (2008). Use of decontextualized talk across story contexts: How oral storytelling and emergent reading can scaffold children's development. *Early Education & Development, 19,* 161–187.

Dickinson, C. (1991). Teaching agenda and setting: Constraints on conversation in preschools. In A. McCabe & C. Peterson (Eds), *Developing narrative structure* (pp. 255–303). Hillsdale, NJ: Lawrence Erlbaum Associates.

Empson, W. (1930) *Seven types of ambiguity: A study of its effects on English verse.* London: Chatto & Windus.

Fox, C. (1993). *At the very edge of the forest: the influence of literature on storytelling by children.* London: Cassell.

Griffin, T., Hemphill, L., Camp, L. & Wolf, D. (2004) Oral discourse in the preschool years and later literacy skills. *First Language, 24,* 123–147.

Haven, K. (2007). *Story proof: The science behind the startling power of story.* Westport: Greenwood Publishing.

Heath, S. B. (1982). What no bedtime story means: Narrative skills at home and school. *Language in Society, 11,* 49–76.

Hudson, J. & Shapiro, L. (1991). From knowing to telling: The development of children's scripts, stories and personal narratives. In A. McCabe & C. Peterson, C. (Eds), *Developing narrative structure* (pp. 89–136). Hillsdale, NJ: Lawrence Erlbaum Associates.

McCabe, A. & Bliss, L. (2003). *Patterns of narrative discourse: A multicultural lifespan approach.* Boston, MA: Pearson Education.

McCabe, A., Bliss, L., Barra, G. & Bennett, M. (2008). Comparison of personal versus fictional narratives of children with language impairment. *American Journal of Speech-Language Pathology, 17,* 194–206.

Melzi, G., & Caspe, M. (2008). Research approaches to narrative, literacy, and education. In N. Hornberger (Ed.), *Encyclopedia of language and education* (2nd ed., Vol. 10, pp. 151–164). Springer.

Michaels, S. (1981). 'Sharing time': Children's narrative styles and differential access to literacy. *Language in Society, 10,* 423–442.

Nelson, K. (1999). Event representations, narrative development and internal working models. *Attachment and Human Development, 1(3),* 239–252.

Nelson, K. & Gruendel, J. (1986). *Event knowledge: Structure and function in development.* Hillsdale, NJ: Lawrence Erlbaum Associates.

Reese, E., Suggate, S., Long, J. & Schaughency, E. (2010). Children's oral narrative and reading skills in the first 3 years of reading instruction. *Reading and Writing, 23,* 627–644.

Reese, E., Yan, C., Jack, F. & Hayne, H. (2010). Emerging identities: Narrative and self from early childhood to early adolescence. In K. McLean, & M. Pasupathi (Eds), *Narrative development in adolescence: Creating the storied self* (pp. 23–43). NY: Springer.

Schank, R. C. & Abelson, R. (1977). *Scripts, plans, goals, and understanding.* Hillsdale, NJ: Lawrence Erlbaum Associates.

Snow, C., Burns, S. & Griffin, P. (1998). *Preventing reading difficulties in young children.* Washington, DC: National Academy Press.

St. Clair, R. N. & Busch, J. A. (2003). *Towards a cognitive sociology* (Manuscript Version). Louisville, KT: University of Louisville.

Sutton-Spence, R. (2010) The role of sign language narratives in developing identity for deaf children. *Journal of Folklore Research, 47,* 265–305.

Van Puyenbroeck, J. & Maes, B. (2008). A review of critical, person-centred and clinical approaches to reminiscence work for people with intellectual disabilities. *International Journal of Disability, Development and Education, 55,* 43–60.

Vernon Feagans, L., Scheffner Hammer, C., Miccio, A. & Manlove, E. (2002). Early language and literacy skills in low income African American and Hispanic children. In S. Neumann & D. Dickinson (Eds), *Handbook of early literacy research* (pp.192–210). New York: Guilford Press

Chapter 1

Therapeutic storytelling with children in need

Janet Dowling

Background

I use 'therapeutic storytelling' as a term to describe telling a range of stories that are used to help listeners explore metaphors that enable them to experience a change in perception about themselves and their situation. These metaphors are a way of describing something as if it is something else. So for example if someone were very shy, a metaphor for shyness could be a hedgehog that has lost its mirror and is looking for it. The story of looking for it, finding help along the way, and eventually finding it would be the metaphor of dealing with and overcoming shyness. The telling is purposeful, targeted and intended to support and develop the listener regardless of their level of cognitive functioning. The content is important, but so too are the ways in which the story is told and the multisensory elements that are brought into the storytelling. All have an impact on the listener at a conscious and unconscious level. A narrative is a retelling of a sequence of events as a statement and history of those events. A story explores the emotional and sensory components and relationships of those events.

Principles and theory

Storytelling as a therapeutic process is well documented (Dent-Brown & Wang, 2006; Gersie & King, 1989; Gersie, 1992; Lawley & Tompkins, 2000). Lahad (1992a, 1992b) suggested that using metaphor and storytelling with people with post-traumatic stress, for example, enables them to address the emotional content of their experience without having to relive the actual traumatic moment.

Attachment theory is an important foundation of the process. This emphasises the need in early childhood for relationships that provide security and comfort on the one hand and the scope for excitement and exploration on the other (Bowlby, 2011). Telling and listening to stories is one way that listeners can be in comfortable and secure settings whilst exploring and experiencing excitement through their imaginations in short, time-limited, self-contained settings. Stories allow the exploration of frightening things – to experience the fear and elation, the tension and the release, the joy and the sadness (Bettelheim, 1976). Stories also allow the learning of social norms and the development of emotional literacy (Killick & Thomas, 2007), and bring the promise of hope – that this too shall pass, something will happen to put right the bad things that have happened, but also that if at first you don't succeed, try, try, try again.

Other research that has contributed to the development of therapeutic storytelling comes from neuroscience. Sunderland (2001, 2003) discusses how 'fear kills play and can block the ability to learn and the wish to explore the world' and relates this to the brain's emotional memory system. If a fearful incident has happened in the past, a similar occurrence in the present can trigger the same intensity of emotional response. Emotional memories can be laid down by sensory events that occur even before the child can create a memory he or she can consciously recall.

The brain works through metaphor, storing information and memory as stories describing the relationship between things. From that relationship the brain can develop and build tension, release and calm that can become building blocks of learning experience and feeling safe. The easiest way to access the memory is through emotion, and stories (when well told) create an emotional response. By listening to and exploring the emotional content of stories the listener is accessing their own experiences, even when those emotional issues are too difficult to consciously express. As the character in the story grows, explores options and matures, the listener unconsciously learns about their own emotions, experiences and feelings to help them make sense of what has happened to them, and decide how they want things to be in the future.

Structuring the story

There are various traditional story formats. I use a basic eight-part version of the mythic structure loosely derived from Campbell (2008) and which I find fits most (but not all) situations.

Stories begin with the *initial situation*, in which we are introduced to the main characters and the setting. Then something happens – the *problem* or *change* – which calls the hero to respond: typically, something dark to overcome or a partner to be wooed and won. The hero will then *prepare for the quest* – be given advice, meet helpers, find magical objects, learn skills – or do nothing at all. Then arise the *challenges, obstacles* or *hazards* that have to be overcome to achieve *transformation*, where the challenge is resolved. This leads to a *celebration* of success. The cycle then begins again.

The challenges generally occur in threes and allow recognition of the pattern of events – the try, try, try again, relating to how the brain deals with information. Most folk tales have it – *Goldilocks and the Three Bears* and *The Three Little Pigs*. The first time an event happens, it is registered: 'Aha! something happened.' The next time it occurs it is recognised: 'Oh, that happened before.' And the third time it is remembered: 'Oh yes, I have been here before.' And as it is remembered then the listener starts to anticipate the next part of the story: 'I know what's happening next.' With anticipation comes learning and thus the possibility of change (Dowling, 2009, 2010).

Work in practice

The focus of this chapter is on the work at the Children's Trust in Tadworth, Surrey with children who have acquired brain injury from traumatic events such as road traffic accidents, near drowning or strokes. However, it has application to all children (and indeed adults) who are in need of support to deal with the challenges they face in life.

Before the session, information was gathered about the child – such as hearing, vision, preferred position, preferred movement. I started (and finished) a session with a short song. This 'punctuated' the time and using the song voice differentiated from the talking/telling voice. Then I offered my hand and introduced myself, before moving into the storytelling.

I used fictional, traditional and personal stories, plus helped the children to make up a story about themselves. This was particularly relevant for children recovering from traumatic brain injury, where part of the process was enabling them to create a vocabulary and emotional literacy to describe what had happened to them and how they felt about it. Just being able to name the feelings was very important and to recognise that they were not the only ones experiencing them. The trauma of injury may well leave children in a mental and emotional state where they have no words to describe or convey how they are feeling. Listening to and taking part in a made-up story about familiar characters allows them to name and explore the emotions and then relate them to themselves.

I used the *visual, aural* and *kinaesthetic* modalities at as many points as appropriate – providing more opportunities for the child to participate and process information. Using tone of voice and sensory objects with different textures (e.g. rough scouring pads, smooth and silky material, knotted string, red stretchy material) I provided metaphors for the emotions that they might be feeling, and then introduced the words to describe these feelings.

Parents and carers were asked about favourite stories from the past. Sometimes it was fairy tales (*Little Red Riding Hood* seemed to be popular). Sometimes it was a book (*Harry Potter*), or sometimes a TV show (e.g. *SpongeBob SquarePants* or *Tracy Beaker*). By basing the work on familiar stories we don't have to establish an emotional connection with a character, as that is already in place. The focus is then on putting the characters into new situations where they might feel as the child feels. This enables the child to access their current new experiences and develop their emotional vocabulary. The experiences and memories of the past are used to help them find a place in the present. Sometimes I made up a story that was a metaphor of the child's experience, incorporating elements of their family story; but not quite their family. There has to be enough distance from reality for a story to be a metaphor rather than a retelling of personal history. Most important is for the intention to be clear in telling a particular story. For example was I telling *Jack and the Beanstalk* as a story to address bereavement, self-esteem, anxiety, displacement or transition? My intention affected how I told the story, what words I used and, in turn, what the child experienced. However, everyone is different, and my intention for the story might not always match the child's response. The child would experience the story at a level they could deal with at the time, and that would determine the course of the post-story work.

Harry Potter has much potential for exploring traumatic injury. He falls from his broom in the quidditch match and lies in the sick wing. His bones grow back but very slowly – there is no sudden magic response. *Harry Potter and the Prisoner of Azkaban* was particularly relevant as the background story for enacting and telling new stories that addressed metaphors for physical and mental trauma. The dementors suck all the good experiences out, leaving the person with just the negatives emotions – depression. It is also in this book that through his relationship with the Weasleys, Harry finally understands what a good functional loving family has to offer, and really starts to grieve for the loving family he never had. In particular, the patronus spell that Harry has to learn to use for his own protection could be seen as basic cognitive behavioural therapy. A key part of the work involved enabling the child to find their own positive metaphor – their 'patronus' – to hold back their own demons and deal with depression and bereavement.

Working with children at different communication levels

If the child is able to speak then we can talk about the different characters in the story and how each of them might feel, finding a physical gesture, drawing a picture or making a sound, then finding the words to express that feeling.

If a child is unable to speak, but does have some way of communicating, then the story is simply told, with objects and choices. Some children have gestures or sounds that they use repetitively. I took a gesture or sound that the child produced, replicated it, and then incorporated it. One boy would fling his arms around with his fingers pointing out. I put a butterfly finger-puppet on his finger, and all of a sudden he was part of the story and being rewarded for it; eventually in our sessions he followed me on the arm flinging, in tune with the story, rather than the random movements made previously.

When there is no obvious physical movement or cognitive functioning, the storytelling is more sensory based, focusing on repeating sequences: the same three stories every week for six weeks, then another three stories. This allowed the development of a pattern of sensory experiences using voice, body, words and multisensory objects. That pattern of sensory experiences became their emotional literature.

A voice output communication aid such as a Big Mack[1] was used to record short elements of a story, such as a refrain (e.g. the bloodcurdling "Fee Fi Foh Fum"), that the child could use during the story, increasing their sense of participation as they began to register, recognise, remember and then anticipate – reaching out for the communicator.

Outcomes and evidence: What I look for

Outcomes are related to the child's behaviour and responses, and feedback from the therapy team and other staff familiar with the child.

For verbal children, I look to see whether they are actively involved in the session, and their recall from previous sessions. Sometimes a child will refer to a story that had been told some weeks earlier, wanting it to be retold, or to share a retelling of it, perhaps incorporating changes in it. This indicates that they have internalised the story and indirectly related it to their own situation.

For children unable to communicate directly, and with varying levels of cognitive functioning, their participation is a positive outcome, as is the way they physically present themselves. For example, actively reaching for objects, responding to different physical textures of materials, and vocalising. I watch for eye movements; changes in breathing; small gestures with the head, hand or arm, or even a startle response; and changes in muscle tone from tense to relaxed. For some children the outcome is a change in behaviour – a child who is restless outside the sessions may be more settled, whereas a child who is normally passive outside may become more active inside the sessions. Feedback from staff was used to discover any differences observed as a result of the sessions; for example, being more settled and less distressed, and in their sessions with other therapists, such as being able to talk about their feelings and referring to the stories we had used.

The story of Georgina

Georgina was 15 years old. A short illness had left her with a muscle wasting condition, unable to speak above a whisper, and using a voice amplifier to help communication. She was in a wheelchair and effectively paraplegic, although she had no specific diagnosis. She was bright and intelligent but found the classroom fatiguing. I was asked to see her for an initial exploratory session. We eventually met for 10 sessions of about 45 minutes, which was longer than staff had anticipated.

I used a combination of encouraging her to make up stories and my telling (or making up) traditional tales focusing on female protagonists who initially seemed weak and powerless but, through their own devices and with the support of others, prevailed and became stronger women, such as *Cinderella, Cap O' Rushes*[2] and the *Silent Princess*.[3] They would all experience the same pattern of loss, developing personal resources, and overcoming three challenges before experiencing transformation. Along the way there would be an exploration of feelings of depression which the heroines might have experienced. At various points in the story I would stop and 'wonder' what the characters might be feeling and invite Georgina's point of view. Even though it was a struggle for her, she tried to respond most of the time. On days when she was too tired she would just listen, and I would still 'wonder' and leave space to enable her to be thinking, even if she could not respond actively. This space was very important. To be able to explore some of the emotional and physical choices of the characters, she had to draw on her own experience, meaning that she was processing and maturing her own experiences through the character's development. Sometimes this could only be done in her head, with no verbal input either from me or herself.

Georgina loved horses, and her own stories often featured a heroine riding on a horse – in sharp contrast to her own situation. Sometimes she was too tired to tell herself, but would tell me who she wanted in the story, and what the problem was. I would follow my version of the mythic structure in making up the story, and at appropriate points I would ask her what happened next, or give her a choice of two possibilities that she could signal with her eyes if necessary. We generally finished the sessions with a recap of the main points of the story, highlighting her comments and contributions.

The staff regularly commented that she looked forward to our sessions and was disappointed if I could not attend. They felt the sessions were supporting her and that she was more relaxed after them. Indeed, she actively chose to come to our session rather than attend the Christmas show.

Georgina eventually returned home after various treatments that enabled her to build up her strength and manage on a day-to-day basis. I believe the storytelling also enabled her to build her inner strengths, and I recommended a book of tales of strong women that her family could continue to read to her. As I had used a regular pattern of questioning and facilitating her to consider the emotions of the characters, it is my hope that she is able to continue to do that for herself as she listens to other stories

Issues to consider

The work described in this chapter is appropriate for individuals working with a therapist who has had training and supervision. However, the principles that I have outlined can be used in classrooms and with groups of children where stories are told for enjoyment and participation without any attempts to interpret or to force the storyteller's point of view. At all times it is the child's view of the story that is central, and not what the storyteller intends to be the point of the story. The storyteller's role is to listen to and observe the child's responses and to maximise that response, either through exploring the language or by a physical representation.

If you are working therapeutically, a basic training in counselling skills is important to learn listening and responding skills as well as boundaries and confidentiality. Access to supervision is important for the storyteller to reflect on the effect their work is having on themselves as well as the clients. This should be provided within the agency that the activity is done. Where this is unavailable or inappropriate, 'creative supervision' is available to support arts practitioners working in health and social care settings, and professionals who use storytelling in their work (see 'Where to go').

Cultural issues

Working with children from different cultures, I was open to using traditional tales from their own cultures and would often ask to meet the parents to establish this. However, most of the parents would refer to traditional European tales such as *Goldilocks and the Three Bears* and *Little Red Hen*, as well as mainstream TV programmes like *Tracy Beaker*, *SpongeBob SquarePants* and films or books like *Harry Potter*. For example, the mother of a small Arabic boy with very little English said *Little Red Riding Hood* was most definitely his favourite story. Fortunately I used a half-sized puppet with a red hoodie top in my stories, to which he positively responded even though he didn't have the language; he was able to follow the story through the tone, pace and pitch of my voice and by interacting with the puppet.

Try it yourself

Top tips

- Assume that the child is cognitively functioning, can understand a story and use stories with simple concepts appropriate to his or her age and ability.
- Have a sound story structure (beginning, middle and end) because that affects the pacing of the story, and know what your intention is for the child to be telling that story.
- Tell stories that maximise the child's sensory stimulation, always looking for new opportunities to stretch and stimulate ('push' and 'pull') and, where appropriate, their previous experience.

Where to go

There are basic storytelling courses where you can learn and develop skills as a storyteller, such as the International School of Storytelling at Emerson College: www.emerson.org.uk. Other courses can be found through the Society for Storytelling: www.sfs.org.uk.

I run therapeutic storytelling workshops: www.JanetTellsStories.co.uk, as does Sue Jennings (see Chapter 2).

Resources

- Big Mack
- Puppets
- Box of materials of different textures
- Large pieces of nylon material in different colours for sea, sand, earth, rainbow

Notes

1 A simple voice output device: a verbal person records a message of up to 90 seconds, which can then be activated by a person with communication difficulties. See www.ablenetinc.com.
2 www.longlongtimeago.com/llta_fairytales_caporushes.html.
3 www.sacred-texts.com/asia/ftft/ftft08.htm.

References

Bettelheim, B. (1976). *The uses of enchantment: the meaning and importance of fairy tales*. New York: Knopf.

Bowlby, R. (2011). Presentation by Richard Bowlby on the work of John Bowlby at Glastonbury, April 2011. Refers to Bowlby, J. *Attachment and Loss* trilogy, first published 1969.

Campbell, J. (2008). *The hero with a thousand faces* (3rd ed., first published 1949). Novato, CA: New World Library.

Dent-Brown, K. & Wang, M. (2006). The mechanism of storymaking: a grounded theory study of the 6-part story method. *The Arts in Psychotherapy, 33(4)*, 316–330.

Dowling, J. (2009). The alchemy of number in storytelling. *IBBYLink, 26*, 2–3.

Dowling, J. (2010). The power of three: Storytelling and bereavement. *Bereavement Care, Spring*, 29–32.

Gersie, A. (1992). *Storymaking in bereavement: Dragons fight in the meadow*. London: Jessica Kingsley Publishers.

Gersie, A., King, N. (1989). *Storymaking in education and therapy*. London: Jessica Kingsley Publishers.

Killick, S. & Thomas, T. (2007). *Telling tales: Storytelling as emotional literacy*. Blackburn, England: Educational Printing Services.

Lahad, M. (1992a). BASIC Ph: The story of coping resources. In Lahad, M., & Cohen, A. (Eds), *Community stress prevention* (Vol II). Kiryat Shmona, Israel: Community Stress Prevention Centre.

Lahad, M. (1992b). Storymaking in an assessment method for coping with stress: Six-part storymaking and BASIC Ph. In Jennings, S. (Ed). *Dramatherapy: Theory and practice* (Vol. 2) (pp. 150–163). London and New York: Routledge.

Lawley, J. & Tompkins, P. (2000). *Metaphors in mind: Transformation through symbolic modeling*. London: Developing Company Press.

Sunderland, M. (2001). *Using storytelling as a therapeutic tool with children*. Oxford: Speechmark.

Sunderland, M. (2003). *Helping children with fear*. Oxford: Speechmark.

Chapter 2

Healing stories with children at risk

The StoryBuilding™ approach

Sue Jennings

Background

This is an interactive chapter where you are invited to respond to different examples of stories and events in your own journal, so please choose a writing book with a stiff cover to record your reactions.

The telling of stories in times of trouble is not a new concept; however, it is a practice that needs to be rediscovered in our highly technical age. It is both built on received wisdom from ancient civilisations and informed by contemporary therapeutic practice. A healing story may be an old traditional tale, or it could be adapted to address the particular needs of an individual or a group. Some people create their own stories for children; others prefer to use existing tales. We need to be aware of what the story is that a child, or group of children, needs to hear. Children at risk or with special needs may be children with learning difficulties or physical challenges, children who have been neglected or abused, and not forgetting the child who is 'invisible'. Therapeutic storytelling is applying storytelling with children who have a range of developmental delays and difficulties. It focuses on the story the child needs to tell, as well as the story the child needs to hear.

Write in your journal a story about any time in your life that you felt invisible or not noticed by others.

The StoryBuilding approach consists of a formula or structure known as the '5 W's + H'; that is, 'Where? Who? What? Why? When? + How?' The structure is applied in an order and follows gradual steps of learning, whereby each step builds on the foundation of the previous step and moves both the experience and the story forward. Although rooted in every individual's creative capacities, the approach follows a developmental sequence in clear stages in order to build the story (Jennings, 2010).

The StoryBuilding way is used for children and young people to express therapeutic needs in story form, creating stories to suit the needs of a particular child or children in particular situations. However, it can also be used to explore existing stories in order to deepen understanding and therapeutic experience (Grove & Park, 1996). In my own work I do not differentiate between story and narrative, and as Polkinghorne (1988) suggests they can be used as synonyms. I find it more helpful to have a big umbrella under which there are many different types of stories: epic stories, myths, legends, fairy tales and so on.

Many of the therapeutic stories that develop through this approach move into other artistic activities, especially drama (Crimmens, 2006). Stories can be danced, painted, explored with puppets and dramatised.

Principles and theories

Although I have always developed the use of stories in therapeutic work in education (Jennings, 1973), there have been certain moments when other people's work and writing have given me sudden bursts of illumination and clarity. The StoryBuilding approach was profoundly influenced by the work and writing of Viola Spolin and her seminal book *Improvisation for the Theater* (1963), in which she discusses a system for helping performers bring truth to their roles and characters, now elaborated in *Theater Games for the Classroom* (1986). Dorothy Heathcote's work on drama in education (1991) pioneered a story form of drama that combines a structured approach with scope for improvisation. The 'zone of proximal development' from the writings of Vygotsky (1973) illustrates the space between the pupil's known and safe area and the next step they can move towards with appropriate help and support. The extensive writing of Alida Gersie, in particular *Earthtales: Storytelling in Times of Change* (1992), has shown me many ways into story forms, especially through her techniques of 'storymaking' (Gersie & King, 1990; Gersie, 1991).

Sensory foundation of storytelling

Creative play, stories, the arts and their therapeutic emergence, and indeed our social and cultural world, grow from our basic sensory experiences.

Sensory proto-play is necessary for the development of healthy attachments and the expansion of the child's place in the social world. Mothers use stories to reinforce this early sensory experience in touch and singing games. However, the senses themselves need to continue to develop as they did in our primitive past. For example, we need our sense of alertness, our sense of intuition, our sense of fear to as yet invisible danger. Only then can we make sense of these experiences by telling stories about them. I am certain that we need to pay more attention to the most basic sensory development in babies and young children, and not to neglect it in adulthood (see Cozolino, 2002). We need to be alert to infant and child disorders that can emerge not only through lack of sensory stimulation but also through 'sensory overdose' and undifferentiated sound (Emmons & Anderson, 2005; Jennings, 2011).

> *Write a story about your own sensory experiences: are there particular smells or tastes or sounds that you like or don't like? How many of these belong to your early childhood experience?*

Work in practice

What is StoryBuilding?

The StoryBuilding approach is my focus in schools for creating narratives with individuals and groups, as is exploring folk and fairy tales as a means of deepening understanding and facilitating therapeutic expression. It is a way of 'unpacking' a story that can be personal or newly created or that already exists in some form.

The approach is usually carefully developed in the stages of 'Where? Who? What? Why? When? + How?': *Where* is the story taking place? *Who* are the characters? *What* is going on? *Why* is it happening? *When* is it happening? *How* will it all end?

The first three are interchangeable in terms of starting a story – we can start with: Where is it happening? or Who is in the story? or What is happening? – and progress to the other two. However, the second three – Why is it happening? When is it happening? How does it end? – are more complex concepts and may prove difficult for some children with learning needs. As facilitators we need to be flexible in order to apply the StoryBuilding sequence in relationship to the educational capacities of the participants. The Why?, the When? and the How? need to be introduced slowly and safely.

Who is involved in StoryBuilding?

It is ideally a model for teachers working with children with special needs or children at risk, but it can also be developed within the curriculum with mainstream students. StoryBuilding can be used with all subjects in schools to facilitate learning and the development of communication skills. Creative arts therapists and speech and language therapists also use StoryBuilding for building communication and narrative skills.

Children with special needs may be children with learning difficulties or physical challenges, children who have been neglected or abused, and not forgetting the child who is never seen: 'She was so well behaved I never noticed her', said one teacher; 'No trouble at all, looks after himself, doesn't bother me, what a help!', said a mother of one boy who was so 'invisible' that he had forgotten how to talk. Below is a built story about a child who 'disappeared' that I create with individuals and groups who feel that they are 'invisible'.

Why use StoryBuilding?

The built story enables a sense of achievement and can increase self-esteem and confidence. It also has the added advantage of improving sequencing skills and making sense of a 'through line' of narrative. The through line (Stanislavski, 1950), helps the individual experience how one thing leads to another before coming to a resolution. This is especially important for children with special needs, since life can often be a series of events or happenings, without coherence or a sense of cause and effect. As Alida Gersie (1992) states, one of the reasons that we create stories is that we require and acquire 'an awareness of sequentiality, causality, the accidental, the unexpected and the anticipated, the predictable and the unpredictable' (p. 19).

When is StoryBuilding used?

It is helpful if there can be a regular session every week or, for some groups, every day. Bearing in mind that the StoryBuilding process underpins other forms of learning; regular input can reinforce the retention of information as well as the means of learning and thinking. StoryBuilding can be used as a crisis intervention when there have been sudden or shocking events in the life of the school, or in the life of the individual. The built story can help to 'ground' the experience, and the metaphor of rebuilding the wall is a useful metaphor for the lives of children that have crumbled or collapsed.

How is StoryBuilding applied?

It is important that attention is paid to the sequencing of the built story. The idea of stories is introduced and pupils are able to reflect on possible themes during the massage and sensory development which often precedes the main storytelling.

The following example shows how some stories need to begin with simple sensory experience, and have a simple through line of sequence. It can be used for developing trust and reassurance and as a warm-up for further StoryBuilding.

A massage story

Create the massage story on the child's back in a one-to-one setting, 'shoulder to waist' (Jennings, 2004) or with a group or class. A child goes through an adapted sequence with their hand and fingers on their other arm. Encourage the weather noises of the rain and thunder.

> It is raining very gently (using tips of fingers), then more rain and more rain . . . Then you can hear thunder (using hands), and then there is more rain, more thunder; then there is lightening (using sides of the hands); slowly the thunder gets less (gentle use of hands), a little more rain and then it stops . . . The sun comes out (use both hands making a big circle), and then there is a rainbow (using one hand making an arc).

The massage warm-up encourages the focusing of the senses and a feeling of alertness for the following story, which is built on the stages described above: by starting with bodily experience we can engage children in sensory communication that can help build the story through the stages of 5 W's + H.

The children are invited to listen to the story and to create sound effects when it is appropriate. The task is for the children to find their own healing in a built story that addresses their issues. The children record their own responses through pictures they have drawn and receive feedback at the end. However, it is important that the children do not feel pressured to respond – the story is usually working on their 'inner life' through the symbols and images.

> *Experiment yourself with this exercise using one hand and fingers on your arm, and see what you recall about rainbows. Can you recall a seeing a rainbow as a small child? Draw a rainbow in your journal and write a story about your early rainbow experience.*

The Child who Disappeared

When telling this story, encourage the children to make any sound effects so that the story becomes truly interactive.

> It is a very stormy night and there is a lot of noise and movement in the forest: branches creak, leaves swirl and rain lashes against the windows of the house of the forest family. They are surprised by a knock on the door. Their cousin is there, and she tells Mum that she has bought a child with her that no one can see because her aunt was so critical of her that she disappeared. Now she wears a bell round her neck so people know where she is.

> Mum sends her own children to bed. She tells the child to follow her upstairs and is very relieved when she hears the tinkle of a bell following her. She puts on the night-light in a little bedroom that has a warm, thick bedcover, and says she will fetch a warm drink. Mum realises she does not know the child's name. She suggests that the child should

ring the bell if she says the name that is right for her. Mum tries several names until, at the name Mary-Jane, the bell rings several times. 'Right Mary-Jane, we have a name for you.' When Mum comes back with the warm drink of milk and honey, she can see the bump under the bedcover so she knows the child is in bed. She puts the drink by the bed, says good night and leaves the door open and the landing light on.

Downstairs, she looks in Grandmother's recipe book for all the ways to make invisible children visible. She sits up and sews a little red dress and scarf for Mary-Jane and puts them at the end of the bed. The next morning the family can see a pair of legs and feet coming down the stairs wearing a red dress, but no face.

The story continues, showing how small acts of love and inclusion allow Mary-Jane to reclaim her identity.

Class discussion can follow using the StoryBuilding sequences: 'Where does the story happen? Who is in the story? What happens? Why do you think that Mary-Jane became invisible? When did it happen? [time of day, season] How can Mum help her to become completely visible? Can Dad and the other children help too?'

The story can be told again, integrating any new information that the children have suggested. The story can then be made active, with children moving and dancing all the scenes, or by choosing puppets to tell it again and create an ending. The whole group could draw a picture on one piece of paper that tells the story as a whole. Greater learning is retained through the activation of the story, and the children's creativity is enhanced. The session ends with children drawing their own favourite moment in the story.

Write in your journal the ending you would choose for the story of the Child who Disappeared *and note any similarities to your own experience or those of children you know.*

The story of six boys

I chose the story of *Mihai the Shepherd Boy* as a story for a group of six boys aged 7–8 years who had been selected by teachers because of their combination of mild learning difficulties and behavioural challenges. The aim was to enhance their social learning so they could see that all our actions have consequences. The class could also see that it is possible to find solutions through the imagination and that life does not always have to be predictable. The story is based on a Romanian folk tale in which a young shepherd boy wants to hide in the forest to watch St Peter when he tells all the wolves what they are allowed to eat. All the wolves – young, old, families and lone wolves – gather in the clearing and Peter tells each one what they may eat and they appreciate the gifts and walk away. An old lame wolf arrives very late and Peter is at a loss to suggest some food. Then he says, 'There is a young shepherd boy hiding up that tree.'[1]

I chose this story as it flags up the opportunity for social learning as well as providing a strong image of the wolf, and wolves (like ourselves) are also organised in family structures. The fact that the story does not have a definite ending allows the pupils to explore outcome of actions and to see the consequences.

We explored where the story was taking place and who was involved. We did some drama games using wolf calls and growls – being able to tiptoe out of the house without disturbing anyone, being able to walk through snow without slipping, and so on. In two groups of three the boys discussed the ending. One group decided that Mihai promised the wolf that he would look after him, and took him safely home. The other group said that Mihai would trick the wolf by throwing down his sheepskin jacket and then running home quickly. We then explored what might be said to Mihai when he got home, either with the wolf or without his jacket!

The group were intently involved in this story and all had concerns for Mihai's safety. Later we made wolf masks and everyone enjoyed playing different kinds of wolves. The children all responded, were engaged with the story and created their own imaginative solutions

There is no doubt that this approach works; hundreds of children in diverse cultures have been engaged with StoryBuilding and have helped to create stories that mattered for them. They have found positive outcomes for their characters instead of their customary 'negative cycle'. There has been an increase in feelings of optimism, both for pupils and teachers, in settings where teachers have also allowed themselves change in relation to their perceptions and expectations of the children.

Contexts of learning

StoryBuilding is most appropriate for children with a wide range of learning needs and can be developed and adapted for different levels of learning and language acquisition. The approach can be used with storyboards for children with little language (Crimmens, 2006).

It is important to remember that there are some children who have great difficulty with processing sensory experiences, especially children with autistic spectrum conditions (Emmons & Anderson, 2005). A gradual programme of sensory experience can be introduced with stories.

Cultural issues

Children feel affirmed when a story is used from their own culture and equally they can get a sense of surprise with a story that is totally different. My own answer is to create a balance between local traditions and new material. Therefore I may use a story version of *A Midsummer Night's Dream* or *Hamlet* with children in Kazakhstan but also use the *Bored Prince* or *The Foolish Bai* from their local tradition (Jennings, 2005).

Try it yourself

Top tips

- Use physical warm-ups and drama games to focus energy before focusing on the story.
- Choose a story that you know well and that has a clear structure with a resolution at the end.
- When helping to structure creative stories, use a whiteboard to write everyone's suggestions and then select them in different combinations.

Closing exercise: remember a story from your childhood and summarise it in your journal. Remember all the feelings that were associated with it.

Where to go

Training courses are available in StoryBuilding and therapeutic storytelling, (www.sue jennings.com) and from time to time similar courses are run by specialists such as Alida Gersie, Nancy Mellon and Margot Sunderland.

Resources

Nancy Mellon's website: www.healingstory.com.

Margot Sunderland has a range of specially written picture books addressing emotional issues with children. Sunderland, M. (2001). *Using story telling as a therapeutic tool with children: Helping children with feelings.* Milton Keynes: Speechmark.

Jennings, S. (1999). *Introduction to developmental playtherapy: Playing and health.* London: Jessica Kingsley.

Notes

1 For the full text of this story see Jennings, S. (2004). *Creative storytelling with children at risk.* Milton Keynes: Speechmark, or email drsuejennings@hotmail.com.

References

Cozolino, L. (2002). *The neuroscience of psychotherapy.* London: W. W. Norton.

Crimmens, P. (2006). *Drama therapy and storymaking in special education.* London: Jessica Kingsley.

Emmons, P. G. & Anderson, L. M. (2005). *Understanding sensory dysfunction.* London: Jessica Kingsley.

Gersie, A. (1991). *Storymaking and bereavement.* London: Jessica Kingsley.

Gersie, A. (1992). *Earthtales: Storytelling in times of change.* London: Green Print.

Gersie, A. & King, N. (1990). *Storymaking in education and therapy.* London: Jessica Kingsley.

Grove, N. & Park, K. (1996). *Odyssey Now.* London: Jessica Kingsley.

Heathcote, D., Johnson, L. & O'Neill, C. (1991). *Collected writings on education and drama.* Evanston, IL: Northwestern University Press.

Jennings, S. (1973). *Remedial drama.* London: Pitman.

Jennings, S. (1999). *Introduction to developmental play therapy: Playing and health.* London: Jessica Kingsley.

Jennings, S. (2004). *Creative storytelling with children at risk.* Milton Keynes: Speechmark.

Jennings, S. (2005). *Creative storytelling with adults at risk.* Milton Keynes: Speechmark.

Jennings, S. (2010). *StoryBuilding: 100+ ideas for developing story and narrative skills.* Buckingham: Hinton House.

Jennings, S. (2011). *Healthy attachments and neuro-dramatic-play.* London: Jessica Kngsley.

Polkinghorne, D. (1988). *Narrative knowing and the human sciences.* Albany, NY: State University of New York Press.

Spolin, V. (1963). *Improvisation for the theater.* Evanston, IL: North Western University Press.

Spolin, V. (1986) *Theater games for the classroom: A teacher's handbook.* Evanston, IL: North Western University Press.

Stanislavski, C. (1950). *Building a character.* London: Methuen.

Sunderland, M. (2001). *Using storytelling as a therapeutic tool with children.* Milton Keynes: Speechmark.

Vygotsky, L. (1973). *Thought and language.* Cambridge, MA: MIT Press.

Chapter 3

What can teachers learn from the stories children tell?

The nurturing, evaluation and interpretation of storytelling by children with language and learning difficulties

Beth McCaffrey

Background

Stories and storytelling have an influence far beyond their use in literacy lessons. Whilst they are indeed powerful tools in the development of language they are also crucial to the emotional development of children and to the formation of their social and ethical identities. In this approach most of the storytelling contexts start with a story, usually a picture-book tale. Ideas are then explored and developed through a range of playful and creative activities, and they all end with a story – this time the children's own.

This is not a pre-created standard intervention, but one guided by a set of principles. There is no formula for the creation of the different storytelling contexts provided. They are developed from that ingrained habit of teachers of looking out for and copying the best ideas of others and adapting them to best suit their own teaching preferences and the needs of their current class.

Theories and principles

> 'A pedagogy of listening where teaching is responsive to the perceived needs and interests of the children.'
>
> (Dahlberg & Moss, 2005, p. 99)

All teachers are acutely aware that mindful listening – 'listening that requires a deep awareness and at the same time a suspension of judgments' (Rinaldi, 2001 quoted in Dahlberg & Moss, 2005, p. 99) – is incredibly difficult to achieve in classrooms with competing demands on their attention. For this reason I allocate one-to-one time for each child in order to listen to their storytelling. In the first instance these are equivalent amounts of time, but can later be differentiated in the interests of equality (e.g. if a child needs more time to express themselves because of particular language difficulties).

An integrated curriculum with opportunities for multimodal representation

This enables children to make connections across learning experiences and to express themselves in diverse ways. Children with special educational needs do not necessarily need a specialised curriculum, but one that offers opportunities to learn and consolidate in a wide range of imaginative ways and that is deeply enriched and memorable. In developing the contexts for storytelling (which may last for a week or more), use is often made of a range of expressive arts including painting, collage, clay work, mime, dance, music, and puppet play.

The concept of 'playful work' (where adult interaction within variably structured settings extends and challenges learning)

This concept fully acknowledges the essential role of play (and in this context particularly, fantasy play) in the holistic development of all children, and hopes to harness the engagement and intrinsic motivation that free play inspires. In playful work, however, the role of the adult is pivotal – both in modelling ways to play alongside an exploration of alternative possibilities, and in gently challenging and extending children's language and thinking. A consistent theme is that play may need to be modelled for some children as it will not be a spontaneously occurring activity. One of the activities frequently used is Gussin-Paley's dramatisation technique where: 'The dictated story . . . to fulfil its destiny is dramatized on a pretend stage with the help of classmates as actors and audience and the teacher as narrator and director.' (Gussin-Paley, 2004, p. 5). The children tell an adult their story, this is scribed and the children then choose their classmates to become the different characters in the dramatisation. The other drama strategies most frequently used are either interactive storytelling (where the teacher tells the story but encourages group or individual responses throughout) or the use of a 'prescribed drama structure' (see Sherratt & Peters, 2002, p. 77).

Spaces for therapeutic play

All children need some respite or therapeutic space within the busy day of the classroom, and some activities (e.g. the use of sandplay and clay) can provide possibilities for healing and integration that are equally as powerful as a 'taught' curriculum of social and emotional development. Therapeutic play provides opportunities for adults to respond to children 'as they are', fostering an atmosphere of acceptance and trust that is not conditional upon learning or improvement. The sandtray and miniatures I use to provide both therapeutic play and as a storytelling medium are set up in accordance with the guidance of Lois Carey (Carey, 1999, p. 188). They include as wide a range of items as possible, including models of living creatures, people (as varied as possible), buildings, scenery, transportation and natural objects.

The final principle is one that relates most closely to the practitioners (Grove, Gussin-Paley, Edmiston & Fox) who were the inspiration for my storytelling approach (and whom I would highly recommend the readers of this chapter seek out and read in detail) – the principle of giving stories and storytelling prominence in the lives of all children.

Work in practice

There is no set sequence of repeated activities that I can describe, and the suitability of any sessions will vary from class to class. The following are two different story contexts I have used on several occasions with different groups of children with language and learning difficulties, aged 6–9 years, in a special school (McCaffrey, 2009).

Story context 1: Sandtray stories

Introduction to storytelling activity

- The sandtray and miniatures available for use are shown to the children.
- The teacher demonstrates the telling of a story using some miniatures s/he chooses.

- Teacher-chosen objects are cleared away and each child chooses one object to place in the sandtray and is encouraged to make a suggestion towards the telling of a group story.

Context for storytelling

- Children each given 15 minutes of individual play time with the sandtray and free choice of the number and type of objects to use. They are made aware that at the end of this time they will be asked to select some miniatures and to tell a story using them.
- Teacher watches and scribes the stories as told (including as much non-verbal action as possible).

The sandtray is usually a highly motivating play experience and when first used the children are often reluctant to formalise their play into a story – they just want to continue with the action! Once children have had regular access to the sandtray, however, and have become familiar with the routine of storytelling, they can combine the two tasks fluidly. It just takes some perseverance.

Charlie's stories

The following are examples of two stories told using the sandtray by the same child at the start and end of the school year.

> The princess was walking. They came back to her house. Then the lion came and woke her up and that fell and then the lady on the camel went found a fairy and saw her and fly back to her house.

Charlie (aged 7 years) in September

> It's a magic land and things get big and small and the snake is getting biggest and eating up the small things. It eats the little boy and all the balls and the baby zebra. It eats the polar bear. But the cheetah is the fastest animal in the world and it runs away and the snake turns round to eat the frog. But the frog is magic and is very big and there is a giant lizard dinosaur and they try to eat each other up and the frog jumps on the snake's head. Then the magic queen takes her wand. It's all different colours and hits the snake hard on the head and the snake is dead and it goes small again. And all the things go back to being small and they don't go back again.

Charlie (aged 8 years) in June, a few weeks after a dramatisation of *Alice in Wonderland*

Story context 2: Using existing picture-book stories – The Bad-Tempered Ladybird by Eric Carle

Introduction to storytelling activity

- Mathematics sessions about time – using the story of *The Bad-Tempered Ladybird*.
- Class act out the story using the repeated phrases and action mimes for each of the creatures encountered.

- Pictorial list of minibeasts shown to group and each child asked to act as one of these for the creation of a new story (e.g. *The Angry Wasp*).
- Group story created through dramatisation.

Context for storytelling

- Children draw a storyboard for their individual version of the story, with separate events happening at different times, as in the original text. The complete story is then told to an adult scribe.
- Each story is then dramatised using Gussin-Paley's technique, with the children choosing the actors for their characters.

Poppy's story

> At 2 o'clock the happy ladybird was playing in the garden. At 3 o'clock it met a little cat with his friends. At 4 o'clock it meets a sleepy ladybird and a wake-up hopper. 'Hey you! Do you want to play basketball and dance all around to the music and then drum all the way home?' 'Yes please.' And they played Ring-a-Ring-a-Roses and The Farmer's in his Den.
>
> (Poppy aged 6 years)

This story contains one of my favourite images from all the stories I have collected – that of the sleepy ladybird and the wake-up hopper. This creativity may have been forced upon Poppy because she did not have the word 'grasshopper' fully integrated into her vocabulary, but it is nevertheless a powerfully contrasting image. The story was written for dramatisation and Poppy ensured that all the class would want to take part. She included basketball to tempt the boys and Ring-a-Ring-a-Roses because it was the favourite game of her best friend. Such inclusivity and cooperation is exactly what we like to celebrate in the classroom and it is important to note that this would not have been achieved if I had insisted that the main character in Poppy's story should replicate the bad-temperedness of the original ladybird.

Outcomes and evidence: What we look for

Assessment framework

The multi-perspective analysis grid that forms the assessment framework for this storytelling approach was integral to the research because it supported the development of a holistic understanding of the different strands of each child's development. Scribed stories and reflective notes are used to complete the assessment, and for everyday classroom use it can be adapted to focus on whichever elements from the list below teachers are most interested in at the time (full details of the framework are provided in McCaffrey, 2009).

Context   Details about the child and the context of the story; number of words used.

Language analysis   Number of words, sentence level (Derbyshire Language Scheme Manual – Knowles & Masidlover, 1982), T-units (Fox, 1993, pp. 53–54) and P and National Curriculum Level Descriptors (Department for Education and Science, 2001).

Structure   Aspects of character, predicament, climax, resolution, and setting (Fox, 1990, pp. 105–106 and Grove, 2005, p. 74). These are the elements which allow the child to construct a coherent narrative that is causally and temporally related.

Rhetorical   Use of language for effect; figurative language and story language (Grove, 2005, p. 74 and Fox, 1993, p. 73). These are poetic elements which can help to involve the audience and bring the story alive.

Aesthetic   Creativity and impact – the shape and beauty of the story form (Grove, 2005, p. 97).

Social   Source of story material and cultural codes (Barthes, 1970 quoted in Fox, 1993, p. 172).

Reflections   Personal reflections on any elements in a story that do not easily fit into any of the other sections on the grid. However thorough an assessment or evaluation procedure is thought to be, stories can never easily be reduced to component parts because there is almost always something more important to say.

Outcomes

During the research, progress was measured using the existing framework in schools for England, based on levels of the National Curriculum, and allocating points per level. As a rough guide, level P4 (4 points) equates to a child who is functioning at a very early level of development, using a few single words, whereas level 1A (11 points) equates to a child who is doing well for a five year old in the first year of school.

It was apparent that the children made far greater than expected progress against the recent National Progression Guidance (Department for Education, 2011). The average level of the first set of stories was 5.8 (range 4.6–7.2) and for the second set of stories 8.6 (range 7.1–11.3). On average, the children gained 2.8 points during the intervention, ranging from 1.8 to 4.1 (see Table 3.1).

It is important to note, however, that whilst the trend was upward for everyone this was not straightforwardly linear. All the children made frequent regressions to a lower level before attainment at the next level was secured. The individual pathways also highlighted the effect that different story contexts had on individual children and served to emphasise the importance of assessing the work of children over a period of time and across contexts rather than the now generally discredited practice of summative assessment of single pieces of work at a single point in time.

Table 3.1 Comparison of mean National Curriculum level of stories 1–5 and stories 17–21

	Mean level of stories 1–5	Mean level of stories 17–21	Amount of progress
Charlie	7.2 (P7)	11.3 (1A)	+4.1
Emily	6.6 (P6.5)	9.9 (1B/1A)	+3.3
Poppy	4.6 (P4.5)	7.1 (P7)	+2.5
Joshua	5.5 (P5.5)	9.3 (1C)	+3.7
Tessa	5.6 (P5.5)	7.3 (P7)	+1.8
Lauren	5.2 (P5)	7.3 (P7)	+2.1
James	6.1 (P6)	8.0 (P8)	+1.9

National Curriculum level P4 (4 points) equates to a child who is functioning at a very early level of development, using a few single words, whereas level 1A (11 points) equates to a child who is doing well for a 5-year-old in the first year of school.

The story of Emily

Emily was 6 years old at the start of the year and had been diagnosed with moderate learning difficulties and global developmental delay. Whilst she was able to speak in short sentences, her verbal responses were always significantly delayed owing to her difficulties with processing language. Over the period of the study she made significant progress in speaking from P6[1] to L1C[2], which can partly be explained by her increased self-confidence. The underlying language skills may have already been present but lying dormant and unused in previous learning contexts.

Emily blossomed from being a somewhat anxious and serious girl into someone who could take a leading role in entertaining and amusing the class. She seemed to be exploring a new identity for herself through her stories and the way that she told them. Throughout the research period, Emily's exploration of identity was revealed in two ways. The first example of this was her attempt at bravery through stepping into the unfamiliar, which was evidenced in the very first story that she told. Emily desperately wanted a spider to be in her sandtray story and whilst she was clearly nervous of handling this large rubber toy, persevered with it in order to tell her tale.

A second exploration of identity was revealed in Emily's consistent creation of a 'perfect' world without disharmony. So persistent was she in this desire that she replaced retelling with complete inversion when telling her own story in the style of *The Bad-Tempered Ladybird*. Her story of *The Hungry Ant* is nothing less than an exemplar of good behaviour and politeness: 'Would you like to share my ham sandwiches?', 'Oh yes please!' Emily herself was a perfect exemplar in school, but her behaviour at home was very different and conflicts with her younger brother could be particularly intense. It is as if she projected her wishes into stories of how the world 'should be', and how she herself wished she could consistently be within it.

It was completely unexpected therefore when, at the end of the year, Emily left the safety of her storytelling world and laid bare her home life with all its arguments and fears. In a whole-class dramatisation she directed a re-enactment of an argument with her brother, which included a great deal of shouting and banging. Her plea at the end of the story: 'Brother, please can we both stop fighting' seemed testament to Emily's sincere wish that all at home could be harmonious, even if she herself did not always help such a cause. This sudden revelation of previously concealed concerns was immediately accepted and dramatised with relish by her peers, for whom nothing extraordinary had happened. Neither was there any sense that Emily felt uncomfortable about this disclosure; she had come to it in her own time and through her own form of storytelling.

Issues to consider

Staffing and curriculum

When I wrote the 'story' of my research project it involved the analysis of 21 stories told by 7 children (aged 6–8) over a school year. This small class of children was supported by me as the teacher and two teaching assistants. This high staff-to-pupil ratio indicates that this storytelling approach may be most suited for use with small groups in either special schools or mainstream settings. It was particularly formulated for use with lower primary-aged children, although the selection of stimulus stories can adapt it to become age- and interest-appropriate for older or younger year groups. Whilst the approach was devised for children with learning difficulties (and does require that they have at least minimal verbal or other communicative skills) it is equally appropriate for mainstream children. However, it may require some ingenuity on behalf of the class teacher to dedicate this level of curriculum time to the creation of storytelling contexts. These can take variable lengths of time and some could easily become part of independent learning sessions, whilst whole-class dramatisation or interactive storytelling sessions usually take between 30 minutes to 1 hour.

Cultural issues

The school in which I work is predominantly White British and for all pupils the first language is English. I am not able to definitely assert therefore that this storytelling approach would be suitable and meaningful in a multicultural setting, although I am cautiously optimistic that this would be so. The choice of stories would obviously need to reflect all cultures and the highly visual and kinaesthetic modes of expression and communication within the storytelling contexts would hopefully benefit any children for whom English was not a first language. Importantly, one element of the assessment process is a reflection upon the cultural codes revealed in the stories told by the children, and these could highlight both similarities and differences between cultures and provide important and meaningful points for exploration within the class.

Try it yourself

Top tips

- Develop opportunities to listen to the stories that the children want to tell you – and only ask questions to which you genuinely want to know the answer. Enjoy listening and forget your anxieties about whether or not the stories are meeting any objectives!
- Produce individual collections of all the stories that the children tell. They will feel valued as storytellers and the collections will be invaluable as a record of their development – however you choose to analyse and assess these.
- Start developing storytelling contexts with stories that you love and approaches you feel secure with – then start to experiment and have fun.

Acknowledgments

To Professor Brahm Norwich and Professor Elizabeth Wood – for keeping faith.

Notes

1   Early language level.
2   Level 1(C to A) is (broadly speaking) the level expected of mainstream children in Year 1 in the UK (5–6 years).

References

Carey, L. (1999). *Sandplay therapy with children and families.* New Jersey: Aronson.
Dahlberg, G. & Moss, P. (2005). *Ethics and politics in early childhood education.* London and New York: Routledge.

Department for Education (2009). *Progression Guidance 2009–10: Improving data to raise attainment and maximize the progress of learners with special educational needs, learning difficulties and disabilities.* London: DfE.

Department for Education and Science (2001). *Supporting the target setting process* London: DfES.

Knowles, W. & Masidlover, M. (1982). *The Derbyshire Language Scheme.* Updated manual available at: www.derbyshire-language-scheme.co.uk.

Edmiston, B. (2008). *Forming ethical identities in early childhood play.* London and New York: Routledge.

Fox, C. (1993). *At the very edge of the forest: The influence of literature on storytelling by children.* London and New York: Cassell.

Fox, R. (1990). *Language and literacy: The role of writing.* Exeter: University of Exeter.

Grove, N. (2005). *Ways into literature: Stories, plays and poems for pupils with SEN.* London: David Fulton.

Gussin-Paley, V. (2004). *A child's work: The importance of fantasy play.* Chicago, IL: University of Chicago.

McCaffrey, B. (2009). *A story of stories: What can teachers learn from the stories children tell?* PhD thesis: University of Exeter.

Sherratt, D. & Peter, M. (2002). *Developing play and drama in children with autistic spectrum disorders.* London: David Fulton.

Chapter 4

Lis'n Tell: Live Inclusive Storytelling

Therapeutic education motivating children and adults to listen and tell

Louise Coigley

Background

Lis'n Tell: Live Inclusive Storytelling,[1] is a way of telling a story that includes what is happening in the moment. It is an approach to communication development that sets out to promote curiosity, encourage wonder, facilitate joy and invite responsibility – leading to 'spontaneous intentional participation'. This is a term I developed 10 years ago in response to the results that I and Lis'n Tell-trained teachers and therapists saw. Some children taking part in Lis'n Tell sessions at school were responding, verbally or non-verbally, without cues or prompts, for the first observable time in group situations.

Once spontaneous intentional participation is achieved, Lis'n Tell is used to address any speech, language or communication need. Sounds, words and linguistic structures can be introduced and reinforced through Lis'n Tell. Social skills can be modelled, encouraged and strengthened. Lis'n Tell can encourage literacy skills and support educational topics.

In Lis'n Tell there is a key teller, who may be a teacher, therapist, parent or assistant who strives to include any response. This may be involuntary or deliberate exclamations, gestures or words from the participants. The key teller uses '5Rs': 'Rhythm and Role, Rhyme, Repetition and Ritual'. A participant may change the *rhythm,* actions or words of a story chant being shared and these shifts will be included and expanded by the key teller (R1). Props are shared. There are many *roles*, according to ability and interest, such as: keeper of objects, scribe, illustrator, musician, narrator, director, character, eye gazer (R2). Parts of the story that sound the same (*rhyme*) might be *repeated* (R3 and R4). Activities related to the theme, such as lighting a candle, forming a procession or passing an object might begin or end the story (R5).

Principles and theory

The underpinning *principles* include:

- The acknowledgement and involvement of the skills and interests of each one present, be they child, carer, teacher, assistant, or therapist etc.
- The recognition that each participant has a valued and equal contribution to make, whether verbal or non-verbal.
- The commitment to creating situations where participants become experts.

The *theoretical background* is derived from many sources: writers about education and pedagogy for whom key references are listed below. Children need imaginative, right-brained activities that have an emotional content to support their learning. They often relate to images and experience more easily than concept (Ashton-Warner, 1986; Wagner, 1979; Steiner, 1966). They need social interaction to be able to learn (Dewey, 1897). Imagination is a powerful tool that can help us solve problems (Dewey, 1897; Mellon, 2003). Children who are given the opportunity to listen to, enjoy and retell stories have a better chance at developing literacy skills (Westby, 1985).

I have never heard a child say, 'tell me a narrative', but plenty request to be told a story. 'Narrative' is a conceptual structure that describes a sequence of non-fictional or fictional events; the word is derived from Latin. The roots of the word 'story' can be traced back to ancient Greek. Latin is the precise language of law, while Greek is the language of myths. We need both.

History

After qualifying as a speech and language therapist in 1982, I lived for 6 years in an intentional international community[2] with children with moderate to severe learning disabilities. I learnt there that a story works better if it is not told too directly, and atmosphere and voice quality affect children's attention. I qualified in curative education, which taught me to see each child as an individual with valuable skills to contribute.

Two books particularly inspired me at the time: *Teacher* by Sylvia Ashton-Warner (1986) describes her work on finding the words that hold most dynamic power for children. This gave me confidence to work with the interests of the children. *Drama as a Learning Medium*, about the work of Dorothy Heathcote (Wagner, 1979), resonated with my longing to see the children as powerful collaborators and not as 'dis-abled'. I was fortunate enough to visit Dorothy many times and talk about my work and receive her insights. Her method of education through drama, *The Mantle of the Expert*, addresses children as experts, not pupils. This resonated with my Camphill experience, where children and adults with disabilities are seen as having as much to teach as to learn.

In 1990, I was living with adults with learning disabilities. I launched inclusive storytelling courses for them with the Workers Educational Association. Storytelling encouraged them to communicate. I took my emerging storytelling approach into the schools and clinics where I was working as an NHS speech and language therapist (SLT). I was invited to run intensive language groups and to start training for SLTs. This challenged me to extend and transfer my skills. By then I had incorporated the 5Rs: 'Rhythm and Role, Rhyme, Repetition and Ritual.'

In 1994 I moved to Sussex, and learnt the skills of storytelling and the link between gesture, imagination and speech while training in storytelling and creative speech and drama. Then, while working as an SLT at a special school for 4 years, I consolidated and named my approach Lis'n Tell: Live Inclusive Storytelling. Carrying out evaluative research with Brighton and Sussex Medical School's postgraduate research department enabled me to see my techniques in more depth and clarity (Coigley, 2008).

I discovered research confirming my experience with Lis'n Tell, for example the importance of gesture in semantic development (McGregor, 2008) and the effects of storytelling on comprehension (Isbell et al., 2004).

Work in practice

I work with 'wonder tales' such as Grimm's tales (often thought of as fairy stories), creation myths and spontaneous stories involving the children's personal interests. For example, an agitated 13-year-old boy with attention and cognitive problems was drawn to Uccello's picture the *Battle of San Romano*. He made up a story about love, death and reconciliation. Afterwards he said, 'I'm calm now.' A girl with Rett's syndrome was beyond storytelling but was still interested in eating chocolate. We told *The Enchanted Pig* in a very simplified, sensory way. Each time the princess in the story ate some chicken we gave the girl with Rett's some white chocolate, which she ate with pleasure. We narrated and related to her being the princess. Sometimes, she appeared to show pleasure at the sound of our voices gently chanting her name and what she was doing. The girl's father said that no one else had seen his daughter as a princess before. This was an unexpected, positive outcome to do with the morale of the father in the face of the deterioration of his daughter's condition.

I work with groups of up to ten children, with staff support, and may use the same story at weekly intervals or over 3 days or for just 1 day. It depends on the needs of the children and organisation. In a typical session:

- An appropriate story has been chosen and adapted for telling, not reading.
- The key teller 'edges in' using significant objects (Coigley, 2002) and/or rhythmical chants/a leading question.
- There is an 'intro' at the beginning, involving story specific rituals, to build and release attention, and reinforce auditory and visual memory.
- Musical and percussion instruments may be used.
- Sensory, voice and gesture techniques are employed to gain and sustain attention and understanding.
- The lower the attention levels of those present, the earlier efforts are made to involve them.
- After initiating spontaneous intentional participation, the weaving begins of SLT/educational aims and targets into the story.
- The children's unique ways of communicating are honoured.
- Participants become 'co-tellers' in taking on different roles.
- The key teller notices subtle nuances and overt forms of behaviour from the co-tellers and includes these in the story, when possible.
- Destructive behaviour by the students is managed appropriately by the key teller and staff present.
- The more disruptive or withdrawn a listener is, the more responsibility they may be invited to take.
- The session usually finishes with the 'outro': recapping the story and acknowledging everyone's involvement.

The story of a group in a special school

A dark-haired boy of 8 years old, dressed in gold-coloured pantaloons, strides around emphatically saying, 'Never!' A plump girl of the same age has asked him what his name is. He pauses then walks down besides a long white strip of silk. The girl leans over, taking a long, soft object, and puts it onto the silk. The boy jumps and yells. He shouts, 'I freezing!' We set up a chant: 'Freeze like ice; burn like fire.' The girl asks him again, 'Name?'

The boy is autistic and the girl has severe learning disabilities. They have just shown the beginning of the Egyptian creation myth, the struggle for power between the sun god Ra and his wise daughter Isis, who tricks him with a snake into telling his secret name. A girl with Williams syndrome and myself tell the story in turns, piecing the tale together, taking care to leave gaps for action and dialogue. We describe what was actually going on, as well as guide the story. I take her through the three-step Lis'n Tell narrator process, which I teach on the training. It has taken us six 40-minute weekly sessions to get to this point.

The boy playing Ra, who had severe difficulties with learning not to interrupt, waits and listens before appropriately joining in. He refuses to move on at one point, until Isis wraps his foot in a magic bandage after the snake has 'bitten' him. I had forgotten to tell that part and he has remembered. My co-teller turns to me and says, grinning: 'It's going really well isn't it?' I witness the progress made by Isis, who initially would sit and pretend to sleep for nearly the entire session but who is now participating on cue. There is also a girl with Apert's syndrome. She only agrees to use a few signs with her conjoined fingers. She has a lot of understanding and some inner language. We have a problem getting her to listen and express herself. Given an array of props, however, she finds and hands them over at the right time, thus showing or telling the story in another way, as keeper of the objects.

Then there is the boy with Down's syndrome, who had refused to stay with us in the first session. I found out that he loves reading. I bare-boned the story to 20 verbs and nouns and printed them on separate pieces of card. At the next session, I drop them on the floor and enlist the boy's help in sorting them out. He does so each week for six sessions, listening intently and lining up the words. In the seventh session, he gets up and tells the entire story. He has moved from scribe to narrator role.

Three years of almost weekly sessions later, taking part in different stories, the boy with autism transformed from the resistant Ra into Mr William Shakespeare. He became able to tell a simplified version of 'Pyramus and Thisbe' from *A Midsummer Night's Dream*, while it was played out in front of him by his classmates. He had developed from being a character/director to an inclusive narrator, within the Lis'n Tell framework.

What we look for: Outcomes and evidence

Assessment frameworks are varied, according to what you are using Lis'n Tell to work on. They may include:

- Social communication skills; for example, the Pragmatics Profile (Dewart & Summers, 1996).
- Expression, Reception and Recall of Narrative Instrument (ERRNI) (Bishop, 2004).
- Narrative assessments (Leitao & Allan, 2003).
- Lis'n Tell rating scales, which I have developed for recording how to facilitate a particular skill and record when it emerges, becomes intermittent, frequent, reliable and generalised.
- Lis'n Tell-trained SLTs in Lambeth, Jane Trevor and Sue Maughan, have developed simple target and outcome forms looking at Engagement and Attention; Feelings; Thinking and Language, with relevant subcategories, based on a framework developed by Grove (2005).

The following training and demonstration workshops are also available:

- Staff at special schools for children with autism and physical disabilities have reported increased levels of staff spontaneity in relation to their students.

- SLTs have shared their observations:
    - At I CAN's Meath School (2011–12), children showed increased levels of attention, sequencing and memory during Lis'n Tell sessions, in comparison to when they were read a story.
    - Nursery school children in Scotland and Great Yarmouth showed increased spontaneous intentional participation and use of imaginative skills.
    - Since using Lis'n Tell techniques in language groups in Lambeth NHS (2010–2011), parent and child attendance rates have changed from sporadic, abandoned attendance to regular involvement.
    - Other effects observed by therapists include children's increased vocabulary levels; enhanced social skills; social bonding between the parents; an increase in instances of initiation of communication between the children and, as evidenced by the parents in verbal reports, spontaneous reinforcement of the storytelling at home.
- A programme evaluation is being planned with the speech and language therapy service in the London Borough of Lambeth, in collaboration with City University's Department of Language and Communication Science.

Contexts of learning

- Individual therapy sessions with Lis'n Tell as a bridge to generalising specific skills such as phonological processes and linguistic structures.
- Integrating children with additional needs into mainstream classes.
- Classes in special schools.
- Provision for children with emotional behavioural difficulties.

Cultural issues in your storytelling

Stories can help us approach cultural taboos such as dying. An elderly lady taught me much about this subject, by telling me the Russian folk tale of *The Soldier and Death*. I have worked with students from over 30 countries, from 4 continents. Some, from China, had never heard stories. They were children of the Cultural Revolution, during which stories were banned. I have encountered the fear that can exist between some cultures. Stories about Akbar, the 16th century Muslim Mogul Emperor, who was renowned for his religious tolerance, and his advisor Birbal, a Hindu, are witty and wise teaching tales. However, I have encountered anxiety from one group of Muslims, who had difficulty in incorporating a Hindu name. I have worked with an Arabic woman who feels that her ancestors' stories have been appropriated by a neighbouring culture. She regards this as an act of suppression.

In the culture of stories, in many from Africa, Russia and Europe, we find a poor boy, girl or fool who becomes the hero/heroine. This represents the value of people in our societies who have skills, not of conventional intelligence, but of the heart. Each character in a wonder tale can depict different aspects of human nature (Meyer, 1995). Storytelling, emerging out of our deepest human experience, reveals a world of 'magical thinking' (Warner, 2011), of transformation, and our ability to overcome. I strive to help this resonate through all cultures that I encounter; for instance, encouraging the involvement of a teenage Inuit girl who longed to sing 'Blue Moon' at the end of a group retelling of *The Frog Princess*. I was delighted to witness this emerging adult, from an Inuit culture, singing an American 1930s song, in a Grimm's wonder tale which was originally from central Europe! This crossed many cultural and historical boundaries.

Then there can be specific issues relating to education within a culture. Working for the government in Singapore, I was asked to 'develop the imagination of parents'. I was told they feared the academic failure of their children, and put pressure on them to succeed at the expense of their emotional development. Now, in the UK, Michael Morpurgo and others plead for more imagination and creativity in our education system (Morpurgo, 2011).

Try it yourself

Start with children you think may be more amenable! Tell a story that you like and that you think the children would enjoy. Make up chants based on parts of it and use them as call–response. Tell freely without referring to a book. Work at a more sensory level for children with profound disabilities. Include more dynamic interaction for children with behaviour/attention challenges. Watch and listen for any responses and respectfully include them as they emerge. Explore a problem that the story poses, like an obstacle on a journey. Begin and end with some special words or actions. Use unusual props that move, light up and/or make a sound, offer them around in a structured way. Do not correct the children; accept and reflect what they offer.

Top tips

- Include the passions of your students in your storytelling.
- Practise telling stories so that you make it irresistible for pupils with very different needs to participate.
- Remember the reason for doing this is to increasingly surrender your ways of telling to theirs, while inspiring them to maximise their communication.

Where to go

I run bespoke workshops in Lis'n Tell wherever I am invited – in schools and galleries, departments of health and education, for charities in the UK and abroad, special interest groups and at the International School of Storytelling in Sussex, UK. Parts 1 and 2 of the formal Lis'n Tell training take 2 days each.

Contact me at lfc@lisntell.com or via www.lisntell.com for more information.

Resources and websites

www.lisntell.com
www.mantleoftheexpert.com
www.schoolofstorytelling.com

Acknowledgement

I would like to thank Peter Sollars for our conversations and his invaluable insights and comments.

Notes

1 © Louise Coigley 2012.
2 One of the Camphill communities (see www.camphill.org.uk).

References

Ashton-Warner, S. (1986). *Teacher.* New York: Touchstone Press.

Bishop, D. (2004). *Expression, Reception and Recall of Narrative Instrument (ERRNI).* Pearson.

Coigley, L. (2002). *Story works: Language for learning.* Presented at the NAPLIC Conference (National Association of Professionals concerned with Language Impairment), Oxford University.

Coigley, L. (2008). *What hinders and what helps. Lis'n Tell: Live Inclusive Storytelling.* Presented to the London Speech and Language Therapy Special Interest Group in Autism, City University, London.

Dewart, H. & Summers S. (1996). *The pragmatics profile of everyday communication skills in children.* Available at: http://wwwedit.wmin.ac.uk/psychology/pp/children.htm.

Dewey, J. (1897). My pedagogic creed. *School Journal, 54,* 77–80.

Grove, N. (2005). *Ways into literature.* London: David Fulton.

Isbell, R., Sobol, J., Lindauer, L., & Lowrance, A. (2004). The effects of storytelling and story reading on the oral language complexity and story comprehension of young children. *Early Childhood Education Journal, 32(3),* 157–163.

Leitao, S. & Allan, L. (2003). *Peter and the Cat narrative assessment.* Keighley, West Yorkshire: Black Sheep Press.

McGregor, K. (2008). Gesture supports children's word learning. *International Journal of Speech–Language Pathology, 10(3),* 112–117.

Mellon, N. (2003). *Storytelling and the art of the imagination.* Cambridge, MA: Yellow Moon Press.

Meyer, R. (1995). *The wisdom of fairy tales.* London: Floris Books.

Morpurgo, M. (2011). The power of storytelling. *Resurgence, July/August (267).*

Steiner, R. (1966). *General education course: Lecture 2, 1919.* (pp. 26–40). Rudolf Steiner Press.

Warner, M. (2011). *Stranger magic charmed states and the Arabian Nights.* London: Chatto and Windus.

Wagner, B. J. (1979). *Drama as a learning medium.* London: Hutchinson Press.

Westby, C. E. (1985). Learning to talk: Talking to learn. In C. S. Simon (Ed.), *Communication skills and classroom success* (pp. 181–218). San Diego, CA: College Hill Press.

Chapter 5

Interactive Storytelling

Keith Park

Background

A Swahili story, *Meat of the Tongue* (Carter, 1991), tells of a sultan whose unhappy wife grows leaner and more listless every day. The sultan sees a poor man whose wife is healthy and happy, and he asks the poor man why this is. 'Very simple', answers the poor man, 'I feed her meat of the tongue.' The sultan immediately orders the butcher to buy the tongues of all the slaughtered animals of the town, and feeds them to his wife. The queen gets even more thin and poorly. The sultan then orders the poor man to exchange wives. Once in the palace, the poor man's wife grows thin and pale. Eventually the sultan learns that 'meat of the tongue' is story – the poor man tells his wife of his daily experiences, sings her songs and tells her legends.

Storytelling, it seems, is a vital ingredient of human experience. This being so, it is relevant for everyone, including those who have the most profound intellectual and sensory impairments. Jean Ware (1994, p. 72) suggests that in choosing activities for people with profound and multiple learning difficulties our aim should be 'to enable the child to participate in those experiences which are uniquely human'. Storytelling seems to be one of these uniquely human experiences. Whether it is legend, myth, folk tale, fairy story, poem, novel, film or play, the principle is the same: everyone everywhere enjoys stories. According the story *Meat of the Tongue*, we all *need* them.

Interactive Storytelling

Interactive Storytelling began as a way of including children and adults with the most severe and profound learning disabilities in storytelling activities. It can be used with anyone and has been implemented with children and adults with and without learning disabilities across the UK.

The method used with all the stories is call and response; this approach is many thousands of years old and is used in various forms throughout the world. For example, the storyteller calls out a line and the other participants respond either by repeating the same words or by calling out a different line, and so on throughout the story. This rhythmic exchange between the storyteller and the group provides a powerful momentum. It is very simple and very effective.[1]

Within this approach, it is rhythm, response and repetition that are emphasised as a means of developing social communication. The story aspect is the narrative structure that acts as the framework within which this interaction takes place.

The rhythms that are used are the basic four-beat, which Trevarthen (2005) suggests are fundamental in mother–infant communication worldwide. Hence Interactive Storytelling is drawing on the earliest movement and sound responses, which we could think of as the two valves of the heart opening and closing. For example:

> If we **shadows** have offended
> **Think** but **this** and **all** is mended
> **That** you **have** but **slum**bered **here**
> **While** these **visions did** appear
> Shakespeare, *A Midsummer Night's Dream*

In Interactive Storytelling we use mainly poetry and the plays of Shakespeare. Poetic novels such as *Finnegans Wake*, which communicate through the musical nature of the text, have also been adapted. When traditional stories (such as folk tales) are used, these are written up in metrical form such as the Egyptian legend *The Well of Truth* or a South African tale, *Tokoloshe Man*. The same metrical technique is applied to Aesop, Homer, Chaucer and adaptations of classic texts such as Dickens' *A Christmas Carol* and *Oliver Twist*.

Principles

The following principles of Interactive Storytelling reflect the fact that its beginnings were with groups of either children or adults with severe and profound learning/intellectual disabilities. Nevertheless, they apply equally to anyone and everyone, irrespective of disability.

Apprehension precedes comprehension

Introducing their adaptation of Homer's *Odyssey* for individuals with severe and profound learning disabilities, Grove and Park (1996) ask:

> How necessary is verbal comprehension to the understanding of poetry and literature? We know that people with profound learning disabilities can enjoy music, so why not the music of words? Do we have to *comprehend* before we can *apprehend*? Does the meaning of a poem or story have to be retrieved through a process of decoding individual words, or can it be grasped through a kind of atmosphere created through sound and vision? (p. 2)

A good illustration of this 'atmosphere created through sound and vision' is provided by Samuel Taylor Coleridge's *Kubla Khan*, which has been described (by the poet Swinburne) as the supreme example of music in the English language. When read aloud, the poem can seem to be a mysterious and magical incantation (readers are recommended to try it).

> I would build that dome in air,
> That sunny dome! Those caves of ice!
> And all who heard should see them there,
> And all should cry, beware! Beware!
> His flashing eyes, his floating hair!
> Weave a circle round him thrice,
> And close your eyes with holy dread,

> For he on honeydew hath fed,
> And drunk the milk of paradise
>   Samuel Taylor Coleridge, *Kubla Khan*

A second example from 20th century literature is *Finnegans Wake* (Joyce, 1971), the monumental novel by James Joyce, the first word of which is 'riverrun'. The storyline of the book is nightmarishly complex, large parts of it are unintelligible, and yet when it is heard it has poetic prose of great beauty and power. Joyce suffered from eye problems for all his adult life and was nearly blind during the 17 years it took him to complete *Finnegans Wake*. Large parts of it were dictated by him, and in a language that is not really English, but a dream-like combination of many languages. The following extract, constructed out of the last and first sentences of the book, contains a mixture of rhythm and timing that is easy to do, although harder to describe on paper: 'riverrun' is three short beats, while the intervening lines are slower. The music of words should become apparent on reading it aloud. It has been used many times as part of a poetry workshop.

> riverrun
> from swerve of shore to bend of bay
> riverrun
> a way a lone a last
> a loved a long the
> riverrun
> from swerve of shore to bend of bay
> riverrun
>   James Joyce, *Finnegans Wake*

The writer Samuel Becket once said of *Finnegans Wake*: 'it isn't about anything – it just *is*.' A first step towards any construction of meaning might be to provide opportunities for the apprehension of text that somehow involves active participation. Instead of just hearing and seeing a piece of literature, we can explore the possibilities of acting it out and then see how people respond to the experience. For all readers of *Finnegans Wake* (not only those with special needs) the starting point is the feel and sound of the text – meaning emerges through our interaction with it.

Affect and engagement are central to responses to literature

In her discussion of using literature with individuals with severe and profound learning disabilities, Grove (2005, pp. 15–16) suggests that:

> Meaning is grounded in emotion, or affect, which provides the earliest and most fundamental impulse for communication . . . It follows that we can take two routes when adapting literature for students with language difficulties. We can build rich affective associations, using stretches of text as script, emphasising the feel of the meaning. This can be regarded as a 'top-down' approach. The second approach is 'bottom-up', and involves decoding meaning through simplification and explanation. The starting point for the top-down approach is to generate an emotional response to the text.

One day I went into a school to do a workshop on *Macbeth* with a group of teenagers with severe learning disabilities. We turned off the lights, closed the curtains and recited the witches' spell in a whispered call and response:

> Double, double toil and trouble
> Fire burn and cauldron bubble
> Fillet of a fenny snake
> In the cauldron boil and bake
> Eye of newt and toe of frog
> Wool of bat and tongue of dog
> > Shakespeare, *Macbeth*

After the final line, one of teenagers shivered and said 'light on'. So the lights were switched back on and her teacher asked her why she wanted the lights back on. 'Scary', she replied.

Recital and performance are valid means of experiencing stories, drama and poetry

'For most of human history, "literature", both fiction and poetry, has been narrated, not written – heard, not read' (Carter, 1991, p. ix). The literature of fiction and poetry from around the world has existed in oral form for many thousands of years, long before the development of comparatively recent (and more passive) forms: writing, printing, radio, TV, cinema and the Internet. The oral narration of stories was, and often still is, a social event where the story is sung, spoken or chanted, or in other words, performed (Pellowski, 1990). Storytelling may be far more important than reading and writing: our starting point for literature may therefore be, using Grove's terminology, 'the physicality of text' (Grove, 2005, p. 11), or in other words, in performance and recital.

Work in practice

The approach is primarily aimed at enabling interaction – that is awareness and response to others, turn taking, anticipation, gaze alternation, showing objects, seeking physical proximity. These are all aspects of very early communication (Bates et al., 1979). Sessions are generally weekly and last about 30–45 minutes for teenagers, and around 15–20 minutes for very young children.

Introduction   The session begins with an introduction using a number of name games. This activity is a semi-improvised interactive song using four-point rhythm that includes everyone's name in sequence around the circle. This enables the people who are blind or partially sighted to be aware of everyone present. The games encourage people to point at each other – not as requests but to single each other out. Tiny poem stories may be made up for each person, perhaps reinforcing their own 'social story'.

> On Monday Calvin slammed the door
> We said Calvin what's that for?
> Don't be sad, don't get mad
> It's OK to make mistakes

On Tuesday, Margaret broke a plate
She got in a right old state
Don't be sad, don't get mad
It's OK to make mistakes

Main section   This is a performance of a story that we repeat three or four times, depending on the length of the story.

The following story, *Tokoloshe Man*, was written in 2011 by Izanne van Wijk, then a teacher at The Bridge School in Islington, London. Izanne is from South Africa and her first language is Afrikaans; as a child, she had heard the story from her grandmother, who in turn had heard it from her own mother, and so on back down the generations. Izanne wanted to use Interactive Storytelling as a means of sharing her language and culture with her group of children with profound and multiple learning disabilities.

The main part of the story is in English, and the chorus is in Afrikaans. The Tokoloshe is a malevolent spirit or goblin who walks at night. Children are warned that they must build up their beds on bricks so that the Tokoloshe can walk underneath the bed and go on his way. Otherwise it's big trouble! Izanne explained that many houses are built in a circular shape so that the Tokoloshe cannot hide in corners.

In de middel
Van de nag
De Tokoloshe
Vir jou wag[2]

Tokoloshe
Zombie Man
He will get you
If he can

Chorus

Tokoloshe
Bite your toes
Tokoloshe
Scratch your nose

Chorus

Make sure you build
Your bed up high
So Tokoloshe
Walk on by

Chorus

Close the curtains
Lock the door
You think you're safe
But are you sure?

Chorus

Close   A closing 'goodbye' or 'finish'. No props are used in the session apart from drums or bongos that help accentuate the rhythm of the interactions.

The story of Nicole

Nicole was 12 years old. She was deafblind, had profound and multiple learning disabilities and complex health needs. At school she had one-to-one support.

One day we decided to try and experiment. We took Nicole and her group to the school hall, which has a wooden floor, and placed her carefully on the floor in the middle of the circle of people. Then, as we performed the poems and stories in call and response, we stamped on the wooden floor, which resonated and caused an immediate effect. To our surprise, Nicole began to move from side to side on the floor and smile. This was a significantly different behaviour from her usual repertoire, which was an impassive facial expression and total silence.

Over a period of several years Nicole was one of the group that visited many famous London venues to perform workshops: the Globe, the National Maritime Museum, and the National Theatre. Her mother perhaps spoke for us all when she said, 'I have no idea what is going on inside her head. But it is clear that she is part of a group and is gaining from being a member of a group.'

Contexts of learning

Interactive Storytelling is used in the classroom, at home, in the high street and in the theatre. Within the school curriculum it is mostly included within the English, drama or performing arts sessions. In some schools, the speech and language therapist will provide language and communication aims, or the physiotherapist and occupational therapist will advise on optimal positioning of participants for the sessions.

Outreach is also a significant aspect of Interactive Storytelling. Various groups have performed Shakespeare on stage at Shakespeare's Globe theatre as well as at the National Theatre, Middle Temple, a BAFTA ceremony (British Academy of Film and Television Awards) and the House of Commons; Bible stories in cockney rhyming slang at Westminster Abbey, St Paul's Cathedral, Rochester Cathedral and the church of St Mary-le-Bow; sea shanties in the National Maritime Museum and the Docklands Museum, London; Chaucer at Canterbury Cathedral, and street theatre in south-east London, when we discovered that if you are not raising money you can get a street performance licence for free: the group chose to do pantomime in the street.

The participants in the storytelling activities will often be chosen by the school staff. Some people may find it challenging to be in a group and even more so if the group is to perform in a public area. In such cases it is often more appropriate to start storytelling in much smaller groups in school, or even on a one-to-one basis

Assessment frameworks have been many and varied over the years, and the latest version being tried out is video diaries. The sessions are filmed and then analysed in staff meetings to discover what was most effective in promoting communication and interaction.

Cultural issues

The standard format of a one-day workshop in Interactive Storytelling is divided into two parts. The first part is an interactive demonstration of various story scripts. For the second part, participants divide into groups and write their own story or poem. People of dual or multiple heritage are encouraged to think of a poem or story from their non-English heritage and rework that into an interactive framework. This is to celebrate the multicultural and multilingual society of the school and local and national community. These are some examples of stories from different traditions which have proved successful:

- *The Well of Truth* is a traditional folk tale from Egypt. It was brought to one of the sessions by a parent of a pupil with severe learning disabilities – whose first language is Arabic – and reset as an interactive call and response version, using Arabic words and phrases with English (Park, 2010).
- *Tokoloshe Man* is a story from South Africa that a teacher reworked into an interactive version, using words and phrases of Afrikaans (see above).
- *Grama Afabet* (i.e. Grandma's Alphabet) is a poem written by a member of staff from Jamaica, which can be performed in patois (Park, 2010).

Try it yourself

Top tips

- *The circle* This may sound very simple but we have found that one of the most important aspects of the activities is the position in which participants are arranged. Sitting in a single-line circle formation, with no second row, reinforces the group identity and focuses the energy and attention of the participants upon each other. If you try the same activities with everyone arranged in a semicircular formation you may find, as we did, that it is much harder work and that the atmosphere and feeling of the group is quite different.
- *Know the script* Storytelling sessions are far more likely to be a success if the group leader knows the lines by heart and does not need to refer to notes. Sometimes it may be necessary to look at a script, but wherever possible it is best to learn the lines before you start. It is also important to feel comfortable with the words – if you are not comfortable with the idea of doing Shakespeare, for example, then it will be much better to try something else. There are plenty of other choices – Spike Milligan's poetry is a great favourite in many schools.
- *Fun* Storytelling activities should be enjoyable. If no one is engaged, think about a change of content or a change of activity.

Acknowledgement

Thanks to Izanne van Wijk for permission to share *Tokoloshe Man*.

Notes

1   See www.timsheppard.co.uk/story/dir/traditions/africa.html and http://web.cocc.edu/cagatucci/classes/hum211/afrstory.htm.
2   Translation: In the middle/of the night/the Tokoloshe/waits for you.

References

Bates, E., Benigni, L., Bretherton, I., Camaioni, L. & Volterra V. (1979). *The emergence of symbols: Cognition and communication in infancy.* New York: Academic Press.

Carter, A. (1991). *The Virago book of fairy tales.* London: Virago Press.

Grove, N. (2005). *Ways into literature.* London: David Fulton.

Grove, N. & Park, K. (1996). *Odyssey Now.* London: Jessica Kingsley.

Joyce, J. (1971). *Finnegans wake.* London: Faber & Faber.

Park, K. (2010). *Interactive Storytelling* (2nd ed.). Bicester: Speechmark.

Pellowski, A. (1990). *The world of storytelling: A practical guide to the origins, development and application of storytelling.* New York: H. W. Wilson.

Trevarthen, C. (2005). First things first: Infants make good use of the sympathetic rhythm of imitation, without reason or language. *Journal of Child Psychotherapy,* 31, 91–113.

Ware, J. (1994). *The education of children with profound and multiple learning difficulties.* London: David Fulton.

Chapter 6

Speaking and Listening Through Narrative

Becky Shanks

Background

Speaking and Listening Through Narrative is a structured, multisensory, flexible and adaptable approach to teaching children how to tell stories. As an intervention it follows the developmental pattern that children typically move through in their acquisition of narrative skills – working on the individual components that make up a story and gradually combining these elements using a structured framework that children are then taught to use for themselves. Research shows us that even children aged 4–5 years without language difficulties, given the right context, are able to convey adequate information, taking into account the listener's knowledge and organising the content of what they say to demonstrate that they have some knowledge of story structure (Botting, 2002).

Each story element has its own colour, sign and symbol. The signs are based on British Sign Language (Makaton vocabulary) and the colours are consistent throughout all the resource packs, which are designed for chronological ages ranging from 3 to 14 years. The multisensory aspect to the approach is key, as it provides the children with the visual and kinaesthetic cues to support both their understanding and their recall of the story elements. Initially, the individual concepts are focused on to develop children's listening and attending, to support understanding and to extend vocabulary. Children are taught in subsequent sessions how to combine the various story elements together to support the retelling of familiar events and well-known stories, before they use the complete framework to generate and retell stories of their own.

For the purposes of this approach, narrative is considered to be the way in which we as individuals are able to coherently convey information to others about what has happened or what is going to happen, taking into account the knowledge of the listener. Our ability to do this is influenced by our linguistic competence, our world knowledge and our pragmatic (social) understanding.

A story is viewed as being the framework that we use to structure and organise that information. As such, it needs to comprise key components in order that the information given has a context and makes sense to the listener: namely (in its simplest form) a 'when', 'who', 'where', 'what happened' and an ending.

Principles and theory

Speaking and Listening Through Narrative follows the principles of Applebee's stages of narrative development (Applebee, 1978). Namely that between the ages of 2 years through to 7 years and beyond, children develop a concept of character and setting and a gradual understanding that events tend to follow a central theme and are linked both causally and through time. By focusing initially on the concepts of 'who', 'where' and 'when', this approach teaches children to understand the significance of setting before embarking on the 'what happened' part of the story. Once they are able to link events together, children are then taught to appreciate that it is the motivations and goals of the characters that dictate what happens in the story, hence developing their understanding of problem–solution-type episodes.

These components ('when', 'who', 'where', 'what happened' and the end) are a simplified form of story grammar (Stein & Glenn, 1979) that act as a story blueprint within which to organise people, setting, actions and events.

In addition to developing the speaking and listening skills children need to access the language of the classroom, this approach also acts as a functional tool for facilitating children's social use of language. Academic success is one outcome of education but social competence could be considered as important, if not more so, in terms of establishing friendships and being able to function within wider society. This becomes even more evident at secondary level. A final principle of the approach is that it is collaborative – between the speech and language therapist and education professionals.

The intervention is not only effective in boosting speaking and listening skills in targeted children but for those schools who are able to release a member of staff to work alongside the speech and language therapist, they are also investing in an adaptable intervention that can then be used to meet the language and communication needs of other children in the school. The joint working between the therapist and school staff has a positive impact in terms of raising staff awareness and consequently confidence in identifying and meeting the needs of children experiencing language and communication difficulties in the classroom.

History

The approach was originally developed in 1999 in response to primary teachers' concerns about the numbers of children entering school with unidentified speech, language and communication needs. In the classroom this was translating into difficulties attending and listening to teachers' instructions, limited comprehension skills, poor vocabulary and limited expressive language skills. This area of unmet need was highlighted in the Bercow report (2008). It was very apparent that any intervention offered needed to be something that was complementary with, rather than in addition to, everyday classroom teaching. Many teachers reported their concerns about the lack of focus on developing oracy in the classroom and how this was then reflected in the children's limited ability to express their ideas on paper.

The result was a jointly funded project between the local education authority (LEA) and Stockport speech and language therapy department to run a pilot based in six local schools (1999–2001) targeting children aged 5–7 years. All the six schools were situated in areas of considerable social deprivation. Following the success of the pilot study, further funding was provided by the LEA to roll out the programme to all the local primary schools. A further project, aimed at differentiating the original intervention for children aged 3 to 5 years in Nursery and Reception, was delivered by speech and language therapist Judith Carey as part of a wider regeneration initiative.

Work in practice

The following is a description of a typical session aimed at a group of up to six children aged 5–7 years, using the *Speaking and Listening Through Narrative* resource pack (see 'Resources') and focusing on the concept of 'where'.

The session would start with a recap of all the five story components with their colours and signs. The speech and language therapist would then introduce the concept of 'where' by showing the 'where 'card, making the' where' sign and asking each child a simple 'where' question linked to their experience; for example, 'Where do you live?' or 'Where do you go to buy food?'.

The therapist would emphasise that 'where' words are all places that you can go and the children would then have to think of their favourite place and draw it on a specific worksheet provided. Answers may range from 'the park' to 'Disneyland', depending on the children's experience. Some children may be able to write a sentence about the 'where' that they have chosen. Each child would then be given a preselected book to look at, to see how many 'wheres' they can find and share.

Using the 'where' pictures from the resource pack or other sourced pictures of typical locations the children might then be split into two teams for a 'where' quiz. This activity usually highlights those children who struggle to wait their turn and also demonstrates gaps in vocabulary.

The next activity involves a feely bag containing items that are linked to specific places, such as goggles: swimming pool/sea; football: garden/pitch/stadium. This activity focuses on attention and listening as well as categorisation. The children take turns at taking an item out of the bag and saying where they might see it or where it goes.

The speech and language therapist then recaps any new vocabulary learnt in the session and finishes off the session with a story which has a strong focus on 'where'. This can be one from the resource pack, a made-up story or an actual text.

For this age group, the 'who' and 'when' sessions follow a similar format. The quiz games really help to focus the children's listening skills and as soon as they learn that shouting out means that their point goes to the other team, the children soon start to take their turn and put their hand up if they think they know the answer! It is always surprising the gaps in vocabulary that are identified in these first sessions and the amount of non-specific vocabulary that some children use. Non-specific vocabulary refers to the overuse of vague terms such as 'this' or 'thingy'. Learning and over-learning new vocabulary within the context of these sessions supports the children's recall of these new words outside of the session. All the children really enjoy the feely-bag game and as there is often more than one right answer, this game often means that less confident children or those who would typically be reticent about joining in will have a go.

By the time the children have completed week 4 (intro, 'who', 'where' and 'when') it is clearly possible to see an improvement in their attention and listening; they are starting to be more specific in their use of vocabulary and even children who were shy to begin with are willing to take part in all the activities and are showing their enjoyment in participating.

Different types of story

Rather than being limited to specific story types, this approach can be applied as a framework to most types of narrative genre. With young children in Nursery and Reception (age 3–5 years), the most common narratives are personal – based on events that they have experienced themselves. Traditional tales and nursery rhymes are also used. From Year 1 (age 5 years) onwards the story framework can be used and applied to traditional tales and fictional stories as well as being used to facilitate children's recounts of actual events. For example, using a story planner to recall what happened at the weekend. In the resources aimed at older children (aged 11 to 14 years) the approach is adapted to incorporate factual accounts and recounts, and scripts and persuasive texts, with the aim being that the narrative templates can be used across the curriculum to support pupils' ability to plan, recall and structure their responses, both verbal and written.

Assessment frameworks

All children involved in the original and subsequent pilot studies were assessed using the *Renfrew Action Picture Test* (Renfrew, 1997a) to gain a measure of both the amount of information they were able to provide about target pictures as well as the grammatical complexity of their sentence use. Initially, the narrative assessment tool used was the *Renfrew Bus Story* (Renfrew 1997b), which in addition to an information score also provided data on grammatical complexity and mean length of utterance. This assessment was later replaced with *Peter and the Cat* (Leitao & Allan, 2003), which provided a more qualitative picture of changes in the children's narrative ability post-assessment, not always picked up by the *Bus Story*. For more detailed information regarding the original pilot study, assessment methods and outcomes see Davies et al. (2004).

The story of Kamil

At the time of his pre-intervention assessment Kamil was aged 5 years 5 months, was in Year 1 and was acquiring English as an additional language. His teacher reported that he was very quiet in the classroom, struggled with vocabulary and sentence structure and rarely contributed verbally to classroom discussions. At the time of the second assessment Kamil was aged 5 years 8 months. His teacher reported greater linguistic confidence in the classroom, both in terms of his use of more complex sentence structures and having a wider range of vocabulary. Kamil was reported to be more willing to contribute to classroom discussions and to volunteer information. His post-intervention transcription of the *Peter and the Cat* narrative demonstrates a definite use of story structure and is much more coherent.

Pre-intervention

> Peter.
> When he was walking home, he climbed a tree 'cos he heard a meow
> He looked behind him
> When he got to the top, he sawed it was really high
> The man heard the boy saying help
> Then he quickly got the ladders and rescued the boy
> The boy said can we keep the cat? said the little boy
> Yes said Mum

Post-intervention

> Peter loved animals
> Once he was walking home from school
> He heard a cat saying meow
> And he looked behind him
> And it wasn't there
> And the cat meowed again
> And then he saw the cat was stuck up the tree
> The boy climbed up the tree
> But when he got to the top, he saw how high the tree was and then he holded on to the branch
> And then he said Help!
> Then a man was watering his trees
> And he heard Help!
> And then the man got a ladder, to get Peter and the cat down
> Peter said thank you to the man to get the ladder
> Then he went home
> And Mum said you are late
> And Peter explained to Mum and said can we keep this cat?
> And Mum said yes

Outcomes and evidence: What we look for

Following a term's intervention with a group of Nursery children, carried out by Judith Carey and using the *Nursery Narrative* resource pack (see 'Resources'), the following findings were reported by staff and evidenced on reassessment. It is important to note that these findings are typical of both the qualitative and quantitative outcomes from using this approach with all piloted age groups ranging from 3 to 11 years.

Post-intervention assessment revealed:

- Increased attention and listening skills
- Increased linguistic confidence (expressive language age increased by 14 months in a 6-month period)
  - Pre-intervention: 'It doing that'
  - Post-intervention: 'A big goose flapping its wings'
- Increased vocabulary
  - Use of non-specific vocabulary reduced from 15.3% to 5.2%
  - Use of specific verbs increased from 6.8% to 21%
- Increased staff awareness and increased focus on language within curriculum areas.

Teachers involved in the project reported that sessions were practical and easy to manage, leading to gains in confidence and esteem, and enabling children to utilise new knowledge and make relevant verbal contributions.

Contexts of learning

This approach is one that can be delivered with individual children, as a group intervention or adapted for a whole class. It is primarily intended for children within a mainstream setting but has also been adapted for children and young people within a special school environment. It should be noted that this approach would not be considered appropriate for children and young people functioning developmentally below 3 years of age both in terms of language and cognition. Because it is not prescriptive in nature, it is up to the person delivering it to adapt the approach according to the needs of the individuals they are working with. For example, within a mainstream environment a teacher may spend a week on the concept of 'who' but a special school teacher may extend work on this concept for half a term and use appropriately differentiated resources.

The pack for older children has been produced with the specific intention of using the principles of narrative to provide teachers with templates that can be used across the curriculum to support pupils' ability to plan, recall, organise and recount information whether it be science, English or history.

This approach has been used with children from a range of cultures and has been applicable to all. The original pilot study was carried out in an area where a large percentage of the children had English as an additional language and these children demonstrated equal benefit compared to their monolingual peers.

Try it yourself

Top tips

- Think multisensory: all children, not just those with speech, language and communication needs, benefit significantly from additional cues to support their story learning and are more engaged when they can see and feel the story as well as simply hearing it.
- Don't be afraid of repetition: as practitioners we tend to think that children will be bored the second time around. However, evidence shows that the more opportunities children have to listen to the same story, the deeper their understanding and subsequently the better their recall of all the story elements (see Locke & Locke, 2006).
- Remember to move at the child's pace and don't be tempted to move to the next level without consolidating the child's current knowledge and understanding. The beauty of this approach is that within a group each child can be working at their own level.

Where to go

- For training courses in using the Nursery, Reception and Key Stage 1 narrative packs please contact Judith Carey, speech and language therapist, at: Judith.Carey@nhs.net.
- For advice on implementing any of the narrative resources, setting up a whole-school approach, problem solving and training please contact Bec Shanks at: becshanks@hotmail.com.

Resources

The following resource packs are available from Black Sheep Press at: www.blacksheeppress.co.uk.

Ages 3–4 Nursery – Carey, J., Broughton, H., Shanks, B. & Rippon, H. (2002). *Nursery narrative.*

Ages 4–5 Reception – Carey, J., Shanks, B. & Rippon, H. (2002). *Reception narrative.*

Ages 5–7 (KS 1) – Shanks, B. & Rippon, R. (2003). *Speaking and listening through narrative: A pack of activities and ideas* (2nd ed.).

Ages 7–11 (KS 2) – Apparicio, V., Shanks, B. & Rippon, H. (2007). *From oral to written narrative.*
Ages 11–14 (KS 3–4) – Shanks, B. & ICAN (2011). *Secondary talk narrative resources.*

References

Applebee, A. (1978). *The child's concept of story.* Chicago, IL: University of Chicago Press.

Bercow, J. (2008). *The Bercow report: A review of services for children and young people (0–19) with speech, language and communication needs.* London: Department for Children, Schools and Families.

Botting, N. (2002). Narrative as a tool for the assessment of linguistic and pragmatic impairments. *Child Language Teaching and Therapy, 18(1),* 1–21.

Davies, K., Davies, P. & Shanks, B. (2004). Improving narrative skills in young children with delayed language development. *Educational Review, 56(3),* 271–286.

Leitao, S. & Allan, L. (2003). *Peter and the cat, narrative assessment.* Keighley, W. Yorkshire: Black Sheep Press.

Locke, A. & Locke, D. (2006). *One step at a time: A structured programme for teaching spoken language in nurseries and schools.* Gosport, Hants: Ashford Colour Press.

Renfrew, C.E. (1997a). *Action Picture Test.* Milton Keynes: Speechmark.

Renfrew, C.E. (1997b). *The Bus Story Test.* Milton Keynes: Speechmark.

Stein, N. & Glenn, C. (1979). An analysis of story comprehension in elementary school children. In Freedle, R. (Ed.), *New Directions in Discourse Processing* (pp. 53–120). Norwood, NJ: Ablex.

Chapter 7

Using narratives to enhance language and communication in secondary school students

Victoria Joffe

This chapter describes the Enhancing Language and Communication in Secondary Schools (ELCISS) programme based on a research project funded by the Nuffield Foundation.

Background

The adolescent period is a significant transition, typified by changes in all aspects of development, including language (Moshman, 1999). Even though most children have acquired the basic foundations of their target language by the age of 3 years, it is well accepted that language development does not stop at this point but develops in complexity throughout adolescence (Nippold, 2007), when growth is more subtle and gradual, but no less significant. As children move from primary to secondary school, their interactions typically become more peer-focused, and they are required to negotiate the many new challenges of secondary school: multiple teaching styles, an increasingly complex education curriculum, the need for abstract reasoning and idiomatic understanding, heavy reliance on the written word, the ability to take the perspectives of others and a greater need for independent working and self-reflection.

These are challenges for all young people, but for those with speech, language and communication difficulties (SLCD), they can present as insurmountable barriers to educational success and social and emotional stability:

> Secondary schools have been ignored for a long time. There is very little outside help for students with language problems. You really have to have huge problems, be at the very bottom, to get any help at all, and even then it is very little.

> *Carrie, secondary school special educational needs coordinator*

These words express the feelings and concerns of many teachers, speech and language therapists (SLTs) and parents, and reflect the limited specialist support available in secondary school. The picture she paints is reinforced by a review of speech and language therapy services which concluded that 'services tended to "disappear" over time, especially . . . on transfer to secondary school. Indeed we found minimal evidence of services for young people at secondary school and beyond.' (Bercow, 2008, p. 37).

This reduction in support may lead one to believe that early SLCD are remediated or improve once children reach secondary school. Whilst this may be the case for some, consistent research has shown that for many children, their SLCD are persistent and continue into adolescence and even adulthood (Johnson et al., 2010; Snowling et al., 2001). Some research suggests that 10% of young people will show some problems in school with language and/or communication (Nippold, 2010a). Furthermore, the language and communication difficulties they encounter can lead to problems with literacy, educational attainment, behaviour, self-esteem and social and emotional functioning (Durkin & Conti-Ramsden, 2010; Joffe & Black, 2012; Johnson et al., 2010; Snowling et al., 2006; Snowling et al., 2001).

However, it is not too late to support the older child with SLCD (Nippold, 2010b). The challenge is to find the right contexts, partnerships and materials to do so.

History

My interest was ignited by the students themselves, and by their parents and teachers. I became aware, as my clients progressed through preschool and primary, how little support they were given in their secondary schools. As their parents and teachers looked to me for advice, I became increasingly aware of the chasm that existed in the literature, research and resources for the older student with SLCD. The unsuitability of many of the areas targeted for therapeutic intervention, their apparent lack of relevance to the lives of the young people and the juvenile nature of the materials encouraged me to explore a different mode of support for this group.

In 2005, a grant from Afasic[1] provided us with the opportunity to trial two intervention programmes with secondary school students with SLCD: narrative and vocabulary enrichment. We wanted to target areas that would facilitate access to all subjects of the curriculum, as well as support students in building friendships, both in and out of school. Stories and words are prominent across the whole curriculum and when observing the young people, it seemed to be that the skills that distinguished students were the ability to weave together words creatively and tell a coherent story, to hold the attention of their peers and adults, and express themselves as confident communicators. These appeared to be the very same skills that our students with SLCD were struggling to master.

The work on this initial pilot project helped us recognise the need for resources specifically for this older age group, and raised our awareness of the accumulation of negative experiences that older children with SLCD face, and how critical it is to ignite their interest and engage them in the programme as active collaborative partners. We also wanted to support the generalisation of any new skills to the classroom and home, and to do this we needed to widen the therapeutic partnership and invite school staff to deliver the intervention in collaboration with SLTs. These insights and experiences shaped the development of the ELCISS programmes, one to enrich vocabulary (Joffe, 2011a), and one to develop narrative (Joffe, 2011b).

Theory and principles

The ELCISS narrative programme creates awareness in the young people of the role of narratives and supports them through a graded and developmental set of 21 session plans, to be active listeners to stories and to become powerful, reflective and engaging storytellers. It is through the process of storytelling that language, communication and social interaction skills are enhanced.

The principles are drawn from intentional, explicit and student-centred learning, where the student plays an active and influential role in the development and progression of the intervention, is made explicitly aware of its aims, and sets and evaluates his or her own learning objectives (Freebody et al., 1995; Edwards-Groves, 1998).

The narrative intervention is a flexible multidimensional approach. It includes a range of strategies and frameworks to support the students during the storytelling process (Vygotsky, 1978).

Each participant is encouraged to start at wherever they feel most comfortable. For some, this may involve no storytelling at all, but active listening to the stories being shared, evaluating them and asking appropriate questions. For others, their storytelling journey may begin with retelling a picture story sequence, moving to retelling a story from a favourite film or book and then to generating their own story – first told in tandem with another group member and then recounted on their own.

Emphasis is placed on the key features of active listening and storytelling, and the act of storytelling is viewed as an interactional two-way or group process. The component skills of listening and storytelling are identified, broken down and made explicit to the participants in order to support their own mastery of the process.

Narratives and stories are used interchangeably in this programme and are viewed as an organised framework through which the young people can express themselves, both verbally and non-verbally. Stories have a definite structure and are sequentially organised into related units (Naremore et al., 1995). This organisational framework is used as a key support tool to help shape the production and evaluation of stories. Stein and Glenn's (1979) story grammar framework is adapted in this programme through the use of a story planner consisting of the following story grammar elements: *beginning* – setting (character, time, place); *middle* – episode (what happens?, immediate response, action, reaction) and *end* – outcome (result, messsage).

Storytelling draws upon a range of complex cognitive and linguistic skills (Naremore et al., 1995; Nippold, 2007), and the programme supports the expansion and development of language at the level of phonology, morphology, syntax, semantics, vocabulary and pragmatics. The intervention highlights for students the power and fun of language through stories and characterisations. Robust discussions, for example, are held about the famous Dahl characters Augustus Gloop and Verruca Salt, from *Charlie and the Chocolate Factory*, and intriguing debates ensue about the connection between names, characters and personality, and the power of language to create stark and deeply ingrained images. The themes of the programme are drawn from subjects in the curriculum as well as the interests of the participants; thus there is a strong educational component.

Narrative ability plays a significant role in the social and emotional development of students (Boudreau, 2008). Stories can act as a means of connecting students to their peers and as a gateway to peer acceptance, the development of new friendships and a greater understanding of world events (Mello, 2001). The programme encourages students to evaluate the world around them and to express how they see themselves in this world.

One activity, for example, involves students sharing past, present and future auto-biographies, which provide opportunities for increasing awareness of family, culture and heritage, self-reflection and realistic future goal planning. One boy changed his future story from being a professional footballer to working in maintenance at his favourite football club. Thus the programme has an important socio-emotional component.

The approach is collaborative, being delivered by teaching assistants (TAs) and supported by SLTs. Participants are given a homework task, which they themselves called 'Mission to Achieve', to be completed in the classroom and at home and involving teachers and families.

Work in practice

A typical session starts with a group greeting and revision. Students then share their 'Mission to Achieve' task and the trainer provides feedback and facilitates discussion. Every session finishes with a summary, revision and preparation for their next 'Mission to Achieve'.

The following is a description of a midway session focusing on characterisation, with activities listed in order.

1. Revise components from the story planner covered in the previous session.
2. Identify students' heroes, with reasons for their choices and discuss with group.
3. Describe their hero. Students are encouraged to provide rich and detailed descriptions using the character word map, which includes details about physical appearance, personality, mood, thoughts, feelings, use of language and behaviour.
4. Share the biographical story of their hero using the story planner. Students have already covered the differences between fiction, non-fiction and biography.
5. Develop three questions to ask their heroes. This task enhances their use of appropriate questioning.
6. Share a personal narrative. Students tell a personal story about something difficult in their lives but have the opportunity to change one aspect of the story and get a different outcome.
7. Provide biographical portrayals of curriculum-based characters to support generalisation of new skills to the classroom.
8. Revise the session.
9. Mission to Achieve: Develop a biographical portrayal of a character the student is learning about in class using the story planner and character word map.

Outcomes and evidence: What we look for

Assessment frameworks

The research programme incorporated both standardised and non-standardised assessments of language and storytelling. It is important to use a combination of the two, as standardised tests provide information on how the student is performing in relation to their peers. However, they are not always sensitive enough to pick up subtle changes in performance.

We used a range of tasks to identify progress in both the linguistic and narrative quality aspects of storytelling. Materials used to generate stories included sequence stories, a picture description activity and a range of six random objects, three of which the students were required to use to tell their story. We also devised a 'narrative checklist task', which investigated explicit understanding of stories; for example, key components of a story, requirements for active listening and examples of story genres.

The story planner can also be used to assess storytelling by identifying the key components of the story that the child has included. Language can also be measured by measuring mean length of utterance and counting the number of adjectives, adverbs or more complex sentences used.

It is also important to get the perspective of the students, their teachers and parents, and we are currently piloting a new tool, Measuring Outcomes Across Time[2] (MOAT), to do this. The programme incorporates 'My Learning Profile', which students complete at the start and end of the programme and which captures those areas they feel have developed most and those that require further improvement.

Outcomes

Our findings from the randomised control intervention study of 358 12-year-old students with SLCD suggest that the narrative intervention was effective at improving storytelling skills. Whilst no significant differences were found on the standardised storytelling or language tests, significant differences were found on a range of non-standardised storytelling measures. Students who participated in the narrative intervention performed better on measures of narrative than the control group (who received no training) post-intervention. Significant improvements were noted in the active process of telling stories (measured by a range of storytelling tasks), as well as in the explicit understanding of narratives (measured by the narrative checklist – see 'Assessment frameworks').

Feedback has been collected from a range of people, including students, SLTs, TAs, teachers and representatives from local authorities. The comments reflect the potential strengths of the programme in developing the language, educational and social and emotional abilities of young people with SLCD.

The students reported benefits in the areas of language ability: 'I really liked the storytelling best, it helps me with my talking and I hope we are going to do it again' and 'It helped me to bring out my language properly and I enjoyed it too'; and self-esteem and social skills: 'I felt confident and started socialising more' and 'Didn't have to worry about getting something wrong.' Other students reported that 'I used to feel nervous but now I can express myself much more', 'I thought it was good because it taught me to concentrate and listen more' and 'It was really good and now I am able to understand more and have more confidence when I am talking to people.'

The teachers' comments reflected positive impacts on the students, TAs and the school as a whole; for example, an assistant head teacher observed:

> the . . . students . . . have made outstanding progress in their literacy skills which has impacted in their attainment across all curriculum areas . . . The TA trained to deliver the speech and language interventions has benefited in terms of her ability to impact on the learning of students in addition to progressing in her own professional development.

Another deputy special educational needs coordinator noted:

> Each student has absolutely loved being part of the project and they often come and ask when it is their turn again . . . The strategies taught in the small groups . . . were useful and easily applied in all their lessons. The parents have fully supported this project and we have received excellent feedback from all of them . . . They have all commented on the confidence their children have gained and the enjoyment they have experienced throughout each session.

All the TAs reported feeling significantly more empowered to support students with SLCD in the classroom; for example, 'The training has given me the knowledge and understanding to effectively support students with language and communication impairments' and 'Not only has this project helped the children taking part I feel it has helped all the children I support in lessons.'

The story of Himansu

At the start of the project, Himansu was 12 years 3 months and in Year 7. He was eligible for free school meals and was exposed to three languages at home: English, Urdu and Punjabi. Himansu scored below average in his Year 6 national standard assessment test in English. He presented with mild difficulties in receptive language and more pronounced difficulties in the expression of language.

Himansu was randomly assigned to the narrative intervention group. He was required to tell a story using at least three of the following six objects provided: mobile phone, handcuffs, car, camera, horse, feather.

Pre-intervention

> The story is about um police are on horses just taking the horses around and then er they catch a man which is driving too fast, speeding and then they find out his number plate then they take a picture with this camera and then um they use phones to call the taxi people if like they're going the other way and then um they the people get out the car and then the police run after them. They handcuff them then the car's just there because it was stolen from somebody and the feather was and the feather just dropped from the sky.

Post-intervention

> On one rainy day there was a man called Jack. Jack was very rich. He had a wife and three kids. One day he was off to work. He was very fed up because there was a lot of rush and he could not get through all the cars so when he got to work he phone his wife and said I'm coming back early because there was a lot of rush. So it was time for Jack to go home and he drove off really fast down the motorway when a horse came out of nowhere and Jack had to swerve his beautiful car away from the horse. His car got damaged and the horse was in very much pain. When his wife heard about this she was very sad and she told him not to drive very fast on the motorways. So they took the horse away and the horse finally got better after a few days. Jack had earned a lot of compensation and he thought to himself and said I could never drive a car again.

The two stories show the improvements he made in storytelling from pre- to post-intervention in both narrative quality and language. Narrative quality was assessed through a profile based on the story planner and he obtained a total score of 14 at pre-intervention and 37 at post-intervention. This improvement is reflected in his characterisation of Jack, use of story components, consideration of the emotional state of his characters and use of descriptive words. His mean length of utterance increased from 8.08 at pre-intervention, to 11.06 at post-intervention, giving an indication of grammatical improvement.

Contexts of learning

The original programme was devised and delivered to 11–13-year-old students with SLCD. The pictures and tasks have been devised particularly for the older child. The programme is suitable for all students in secondary school as well as the older primary school years, from around 8 years of age. The programme is detailed enough in plans, teaching notes and explanations to be delivered by assistants with support and guidance. It is written up as 21 separate intervention sessions that form a coherent and progressive programme for narrative development, and it is preferable to deliver them as provided. In the original project the sessions were delivered three times per week, and TAs did report that they felt this intensity was positive for the child as it maintained momentum. The programme can be delivered in full in one month, one term and even across a year, depending on the abilities of the group and the level of discussion undertaken. The intervention was delivered in small groups of between two and six students, ideally four to five, as a great deal of the work is around successfully communicating with others and working effectively in groups. The programme is designed to be flexible and to meet the different needs of the students and your own needs too!

Issues to consider

There may be times when students share highly emotional and difficult experiences, and it is essential that support is provided to them, if needed, outside of the session. Students should feel comfortable sharing their stories and understand the importance of trust and confidentiality. Trainers may also need to seek guidance, on occasion, to ensure student safety and well-being.

It is important to ensure the appropriate level of support is provided to assistants when they are conducting the programme.

Cultural issues

Students from a range of socio-economic, cultural, ethnic and religious backgrounds have taken part. Storytelling proved to be a powerful leveller, providing opportunities to learn about the cultures and beliefs of others.

Try it yourself

Top tips

- Make sure everything you do is relevant to students' own lives and experiences.
- Share your own stories and experiences, as this will encourage participants to share theirs with you.
- Encourage ongoing reflection and evaluation.
- Just do it! Dive in and have a go – you have nothing to lose and everything to gain.

Where to go

For further information, advice and training, see www.elciss.com and contact Victoria Joffe at: v.joffe@city.ac.uk.

Resources

Joffe, V. L. (2011). *Narrative Intervention Programme: Using narratives to enhance language and learning across the secondary school curriculum.* Milton Keynes: Speechmark.

Acknowledgments

The research underpinning the narrative intervention programme was funded by the Nuffield Foundation (Grant No: EDU/32220). The author is indebted to the research team, including Nita Madhani, Francesca Parker, Emma Dean, Eleni Kotta, Elena Revelas and Clare Forder, as well as many other students who assisted with the project. The author would like to thank the 21 TAs who participated in the project, together with the teachers and other staff from the 21 schools. Sarah Raymond gave valuable help in identifying case studies for use in the chapter, and Nicola Grove provided encouragement and excellent editorial assistance. Final and most important thanks go to all the secondary school students who participated in the programme, and to their parents for giving their consent. It was a joy and privilege to work with them all. Their stories, and the enthusiasm and passion with which they shared them, have enriched all our lives.

Notes

1 Afasic is a national charity supporting parents and carers of children with speech, language and communication difficulties.
2 The MOAT is being developed in collaboration with Nabiah Sohail and will be available from Speechmark Publishing in 2013.

References

Bercow, J. (2008). *The Bercow Report: A review of services for children and young people (0–19) with speech, language and communication needs.* London: Department for Children, Schools and Families.

Boudreau, D. (2008). Narrative abilities: Advances in research and implications for clinical practice. *Topics in Language Disorders, 28(2),* 99–114.

Durkin, K. & Conti-Ramsden, G. (2010). Young people with specific language impairment: A review of social and emotional functioning in adolescence. *Child Language Teaching and Therapy, 26(2),* 105–121.

Edwards-Groves, C. J. (1998). *The reconceptualisation of classroom events as structured lessons: Documenting changing the teaching of literacy in the primary school.* Unpublished doctoral thesis: Griffith University.

Freebody, P., Ludwig, C. & Gunn, S. (1995). *The literacy practices in and out of schools in low socio-economic urban communities.* Canberra, Australia: Commonwealth Department of Employment, Education and Training.

Joffe, V. L. (2011a). *Vocabulary enrichment intervention programme.* Milton Keynes: Speechmark.

Joffe, V. L. (2011b). *Narrative intervention programme: Using narratives to enhance language and learning across the secondary school curriculum.* Milton Keynes: Speechmark.

Joffe, V. L. & Black, E. (2012). Social, emotional and behavioural functioning of mainstream secondary school students with low academic and language performance: Perspectives from students, teachers and parents. *Language, Speech and Hearing Services in Schools.* Published online ahead of print 23rd July 2012 at: http://lshss.asha.org/cgi/rapidpdf/0161-1461_2012_11-0088v1.

Johnson, C. J., Beitchman, J. H. & Brownlie, E. B. (2010). Twenty-year follow-up of children with and without speech-language impairments: Family, educational, occupational, and quality of life outcomes. *American Journal of Speech Language Pathology, 19,* 51–65.

Mello, R. (2001). The power of storytelling: How oral narrative influences children's relationships in classrooms. *International Journal of Education and the Arts, 2(1).* Available at: http://www.ijea.org/v2n1/ [accessed April 2012].

Naremore, R., Densmore, A. & Harman, D. (1995). *Language intervention with school-aged children: Conversation, narrative and text.* San Diego, CA: Singular Publishing Group.

Nippold, M. (2007). *Later language development: School-age children, adolescents, and young adults.* Austin, TX: Pro-Ed.

Nippold, M. (2010a). *Language sampling with adolescents.* San Diego, CA: Plural Publishing.

Nippold, M (2010b). It's NOT too late to help adolescents succeed in school. *Language, Speech and Hearing Services in Schools, 41,* 137–138.

Moshman, D. (1999). *Adolescent psychological development: Rationality, morality and identity.* Mahwah, NJ: LEA Publishers.

Snowling, M. J., Adams, J. W., Bishop, D. V. M., & Stothard, S.E. (2001). Educational attainments of school leavers with preschool history of speech-language impairments. *International Journal of Language and Communication Disorders, 36(2),* 173–183.

Snowling, M. J., Bishop, D. V. M., Stothard, S. E., Chipchase, B., & Kaplan, C. (2006). Psychosocial outcomes at 15 years of children with a preschool history of speech-language impairment. *Journal of Child Psychology and Psychiatry, 47(8),* 759–765.

Stein, N. & Glenn, C. (1979). An analysis of story comprehension in elementary school children. In R. Freedle (Ed.), *New directions in discourse processing* (pp. 53–120). Norwood, NJ: Ablex.

Vygotsky, L. (1978). *Mind in society.* Cambridge, MA: Harvard University Press.

Chapter 8

Learning to Tell
Teaching the skills of community storytelling

Nicola Grove

Background

This chapter describes the development of a training course in community storytelling designed for (and in collaboration with) people with learning and communication difficulties.

History

The idea for the project grew from a storytelling group which ran in north London for a year, with nine verbal individuals. They all enjoyed the experience of telling all sorts of stories: traditional, fictional (*Wizard of Oz*) and personal – memories of the war and of childhood exploits (Grove, 2004). Funding was then secured to take this work forward and explore the possibility of a storytelling company who could go out and run workshops, perform at festivals and events, and find new ways of making familiar tales relevant and meaningful.

Together we worked out what we meant by a story – it had to have a 'sparkle' in it, something to catch and hold the attention of an audience – more than a list of what happened, when and where. So a story, in this course, is defined as a sequence of events about something which is of interest. We experimented with ways of drawing 'story', using circles, hills and journeys. And when we reflected on our storytelling skills, we always came back to the idea of the sparkle in the story – the crest of the hill, the sunburst, the climax, the unforeseen event along the route.

Theory and principles

The principles underlying the training were similar to those outlined for Storysharing (see Chapter 13), which we were developing simultaneously with a group of people who had profound disabilities. We see storytelling as a social process, whereby the arts of narration are learned through valued participation, close observation of good models, and appropriate support. The role of the tutors is to scaffold (Vygotsky,1978) the abilities of everyone in the group, to research and share the rich heritage of stories available in the oral tradition, and to show by example how stories can be told together. We also adopt a collaborative approach – identifying what each person can contribute to the telling or performance of a story, and focusing on their strengths.

Though some people proved very adept at telling individually from the start, our basic approach was team or tandem telling, where two or more people share the task. We found that this increased confidence and teamwork, improved listening skills, and enabled people to reflect together on their skills and learning. Some of our tellers were good at recalling the events but found it hard to express feelings or to vary facial expressions. Others were so verbally fluent that they found it hard to know when to stop talking! Others, who could only communicate through a few words, were good at sign or gesture. Everyone was able to use a musical instrument or show a prop at an appropriate time. As we worked together we began to find a different approach to narrating:

> Our company emphasises telling which is participatory and communal, which develops an intensity of listening to the teller, an atmosphere in which a contribution told from the heart is valued for what it communicates about our common humanity. We seek to make connections between powerful archetypal traditional myths and the lived experience of day to day challenges and triumphs, and to illuminate the importance of the small, the unnoticed, the unorthodox for our audiences.
>
> Grove, 2009, p.15

Our inspiration also came from a well-known tale:

> Walking down the road a boy falls into step with an old tinker making for a village. Asked how he makes a living, the tinker tells the boy to watch and listen. Arriving in the market square he makes a fire, takes a pan out of his sack, fills the pan with water and sets it to boil. Then he takes a stone from his pocket and drops it in. Intrigued, the boy – and a queue of villagers – ask what he is making. 'Stone soup,' replies the tinker. 'Best soup ever, but it just needs – let's see – an onion/a carrot/a potato . . .' naming the vegetables that he sees in the villagers' baskets. Each villager donates something to the soup and, in the end, everyone shares it and pronounces it the best ever.

This story teaches us so many important truths: that a story is made by a community; that it involves a generous process of sharing; that everyone contributes; and that the inert, inanimate stone is the critical ingredient, whose role in the story is created by the tinker – or support person. We create stories together, and everyone can put in something.

The focus of the course is on oral traditional tales: myths, legends and folk tales, and on the personal experiences that these evoke. For example, in one of our first shows, *Days and Knights in the Kitchen*, we told the tale of Sir Gareth of Orkney from the Arthurian cycle. In this story, Gareth leaves home against the wishes of his mother, Queen Morgause of Orkney, and rides to join his brothers at the court. Not wanting to capitalise on his family connections, he disguises himself as a poor man and is set to work in the kitchens, where he is bullied and reviled. Finally, he gets the quest he has sought, and accompanies the scornful Linet to rescue her sister from the Red Knight, having defeated several knights of different colours in the interim.

This story had many resonances for our group: leaving home, working in kitchens, bullying and name-calling, fear of assault, as well as triumphs (the defeat of three knights symbolising the hat-trick in a football match scored by one member) and love and romance. We interspersed the traditional tale with personal stories and took it out to conferences as workshops where others too could share their memories of successes and difficult times.

We guided people towards traditional stories because we wanted to broaden their experience and because, as storytellers, we had a firm belief in the power of these tales to help us live our lives. However, there was also space for members to choose to tell stories they knew well, from films or favourite books or TV.

The teaching and learning framework

The content of the course comprises four strands of storytelling, which are addressed each week. These strands are: story themes, story lines, story skills and story company.

Story theme   relates to the fundamentals of storytelling: What is a story? Where do stories originate? Who are the tellers? Who owns the story? How can stories be shared? What do stories do for us? The story theme functions to nourish the imagination of the group with powerful and resonant symbols, to develop personal myth-making. Story themes are developed through the telling of stories at the beginning and end of the day, and by work on the meaning of these stories.

Story lines   involves the collection and development of different kinds of story, which are recorded in personal portfolios and are chosen by the students themselves.

Story skills   involves exercises and games to practise specific strategies for telling and listening, categorised into four domains:

Structural The who? where? when? what happened? and why? aspects.
Feelings Expressed verbally and non-verbally, through facial expression, body language and gesture, and vocal intonation.
Social skills How to interact with an audience; how to listen.
Language The skills that specifically support narrative, such as developing vocabulary, use of verbs, and story conventions such as how to start, how to end, metaphors.

These domains were based on work on narrative development by Labov and Waletzky (1976), Peterson and McCabe (1983) and Norrick (2000).

Story company   involves the development of a sense of group identity and social skills through games, the discussion of group rules and conventions and the use of particular rituals: starting and finishing, allocating responsibilities, and evaluating how we are doing as a group of storytellers.

Work in practice

A typical day starts with the arrival of group members. Each week, a different person is in charge of the register and for making teas and coffees. So as people arrive, they sign up and choose their drink (it must be said that never in the history of the company have we ever managed to get this right, no matter who is in charge). Then members get into small groups of three or four to share news. This is done very systematically – we found that when we did news as a large group, it was endless. Also, people wanted to tell tutors the news but were not so interested in each other, so tutors deliberately withdrew from the process. The groups are asked to appoint a spokesperson, whose job is to speak last in the group, to listen to the others, to collect the news and summarise it briefly in key points for the whole-group plenary session, which is the official start of the session.

In the whole-group meeting, we check in with everyone by hearing the news. Then we put up the plan for the day, using pictures and symbols. Again, group members take responsibility for this, usually planned with them the week before.

The planning meeting is followed by a fun warm-up game, led by a group member, a favourite being 'Minestrone', where we adopt the names of vegetables, swap places when our type is called ('onions' or 'onions and carrots') and where everyone gets up and swaps when the caller says 'Minestrone'.

The story of the day is shared – sometimes told by tutors, especially in the first weeks – but as quickly as possible we recruit students to tell in tandem.

The meaning of the story is discussed in small groups, and we then work on specific story skills; for example, for the Gareth story we practise changing our voices and faces to express the name-calling and bullying that goes on. Then we debrief from that and mime the sword fights in which Gareth is successful.

During the 1-hour lunch break, students relax and chat informally; they may also meet with a tutor to discuss a particular issue about their progress.

In the afternoon, a second warm-up (or perhaps wake up!) game is used, and then students will work on their own portfolios, using art, collage, writing or dictating their stories to a scribe. The portfolios are used as evidence in accredited courses, and as personal records. Stories that are too personal to share are kept at the back in special folders. During this period, the team who are going to tell the story of the week next time will rehearse it.

After the tea break is a feedback session, where everyone gets a chance to reflect on the experiences of the day. We end with a positive closing activity such as massaging shoulders in a group circle, passing an imaginary present to our neighbour, who must guess what is in it, then change the size and shape and pass it on. Finally, we link hands and say goodbye.

Outcomes and evidence: What we look for

Assessment frameworks

We use a system of profiling whereby people are filmed telling different types of story: a routine event (what happens when you go swimming); personal experiences; a folk or fairy tale they know well (e.g. *Cinderella*) and finally, making up a story to go with a stimulating art postcard (e.g. Magritte's *Golconda* – tiny men raining down onto a red roof). Reviewing the film, we note whether people show any specific skills in one genre or another (the last activity is the hardest, the first the easiest) and how they express themselves – their strengths and needs in each case. This can be used as a baseline from which to measure subsequent progress. The course can also be used as the basis for developing accredited skills in story-telling, for example with the Open College Network (OCN).[1]

Outcomes

All 16 participants on the first Learning to Tell course successfully achieved entry level or level 1 OCN qualifications in inclusive storytelling. Questionnaires and interviews with staff and families showed that members were felt to have developed confidence and improved their communication skills. A key aim of the project was to reduce social isolation and increase community participation, which was achieved by taking people to story circles and festivals, and enabling them to deliver high-status workshops and performances at conferences, in homes and in schools. All but one member of our group had scarcely left Somerset at the beginning of the project; four people now regularly travel with us to different locations in England and abroad. In-depth interviews with course members carried out by an independent researcher showed how much they had gained from the experience:

> When I first started I felt like I was . . . on me own a lot, but when I went to storytelling I then felt like it's being in a great big circle, to me it feels like being in a family of professional storytellers.

During the final year of the project, members of the company visited another group in Birmingham and provided 2 days' training. Subsequently, a group was set up for 12 people over a 4-month period. Analysis of their skills in storytelling, using a profile of structural components and a standardised narrative assessment (Renfrew, 1997) showed that narrative abilities improved between the start and finish of the course, and that, in turn, their self-esteem and ability to share experiences was enhanced (Johnson, 2009).

We also use stories to empower people and to challenge preconceptions and beliefs about disability (Kondrat & Teater, 2009; Walmsley & Johnson, 2003). Through the story of *Peter the Wild Boy* (see below), for example, we explore not only past and present attitudes to disabled people – prejudice, fear – but also acceptance and support.

The stories of Michael and Robin[2]

Michael is a young adult who was 20 years old when he started on a Learning to Tell course. He was already a very accomplished dancer and used to acting and performing on stage, but was not a confident narrator – he spoke quietly and hesitantly. His skills emerged during the course, and through dedicated rehearsals for performance he particularly enjoyed manipulating a large puppet and speaking through this figure. Recently, in tandem telling, he took a strong role and his voice was clear and carrying as he narrated in role as a boy with learning difficulties looking for a job – a situation which echoed his own experience.

Robin, now in his thirties, is a founder member of the company who had a great interest in history and legends and was a keen artist, but only as a hobby. Robin has proved himself as one of our most accomplished tellers, but this is as a result of a great deal of hard work and self-reflection, as demonstrated in his thoughtful reflections on his own progress:

> I've always had an interest in stories and I've always had dreams about stories, ones that are quite true and ones that I've heard from other people. Sometimes I've even made up stories which I think when you make up a story it's like you make up an image of a story that someone else is going to be interested in, and that story comes alive and people can feel what the story is like, they can feel the vision of what the story is about and even feel like they're in a world where these stories can come out at them and they feel really adventurous.

Contexts of learning

The course works best for students in secondary and further education who have some ability to recall their own experiences, who enjoy working in groups and who can attend and listen to stories and to the conversations of others. The course is flexible and can accommodate students with limited expressive language, but to get the most out of it they do need to be able to understand and follow a story.

Issues to consider

Sometimes stories will bring up very strong feelings; you are unlikely to know enough about personal histories to predict how this will happen. For example, the story of the *Children of Lir* [3] involves loss of home, family ties and banishment. Someone listening burst into tears and it turned out that her father had left the family a fortnight before. It's important to have processes in place that allow people to express their emotions, and to have systems for referring on to relevant services. We sometimes took out a session to work together with the feelings raised in the story through art, dance and music, getting the group to support each other. Generally, we have found that good stories carry within them the resolution of feelings and can bring a sense of closure (see also the chapters in this book on therapeutic approaches).

Cultural issues

Culturally, the course is adaptable. We recommend that if students from multiethnic cultures are attending it is really important to:

- Explore with them stories from their own cultural traditions that are significant and the meanings within that culture. This should involve meeting with some of the people from that culture who are using the stories, who can talk with them about their meaning and their use of the stories within that community. Actively research on the Internet and make contact with key storytellers if you cannot meet people directly.
- Find out about traditional oral storytelling within that culture. For example, in Africa there is a strong tradition of call and response, and of actively engaging and discussing the stories as they are told, and in many cultures (for example Japan) song and music are vital parts of storytelling. All cultures have some specific ways of starting and finishing stories, which are useful to bring in.
- Invite a storyteller or artist from that tradition to work with the group.
- Remember to be sensitive to particular taboos; for example, when telling stories about animals, remember which animals are sacred and which are perceived as unclean.
- Be sensitive about using sacred stories. Some storytellers feel that it is not appropriate to use stories which were collected from sources without permission, such as by anthropologists in previous centuries. Raven tales from First Peoples of North America or dreamtime stories of Aboriginal Australian people are examples. An alternative view is that the stories are now out and available, and that the imperative is to tell them for a good reason and in a respectful way. So find out about the origins of the story and be clear why and how you use it.

Try it yourself

It's worth running one-off workshops or taster sessions to interest people and explore the ways you want to work. Bear in mind that the word 'storytelling' carries a lot of baggage. We have found that some people see the activity as childish, equating it with reading, not telling, or may even think of it as lying: 'I don't tell stories', said one lady whom we tried to interest in the group.

Top tips

- Include the familiar, such as pantomime tales, but bring in stories from other traditions as soon as possible.
- Trust the group to find the meanings that are right for them.
- Try to link the group in to your local story circle, which can be found through national networks – invaluable for opportunities of hearing and telling the stories.

Where to go

Openstorytellers run *Learning to Tell* one-day courses, and can also offer in-service training: www.openstorytellers.org.uk.

Learning to Tell is a resource which includes everything you need to teach a 30-week course, with an example DVD, and is available from the British Institute of Learning Disabilities: www.bild.org.uk.

A resource for the story of *Peter the Wild Boy* or *Gentle Peter*, as the Pitt Hopkins Society prefers to name him, can be found at: http://www.hrp.org.uk/KensingtonPalace/education andcommunity/Learning/Communityoutreach/resources/PeterWildBoyResource.

For your own training, consider going on courses to develop your skills. In every country you will find a range of opportunities, from residential to one-day events: use key words such as storytellers or storytelling clubs. Storytelling festivals are wonderful ways of learning new stories and skills and networking.

To find stories, look on websites such as:

- www.sfs.org.uk
- www.mythstories.com
- www.healingstory.org
- www.story-lovers.com
- www.storynet.org
- www.timsheppard.co.uk/story

The Story Museum in Oxford, UK has an excellent website with ideas for developing storytelling using a 'Hear, Map, Step, Speak' approach, which is very compatible with *Learning to Tell*: www.storymuseum.org.

Acknowledgements

Acknowledgements are due to all the company members and to Jane Harwood, Jem Dick and Derryn Street, who worked with me on the development of the course, and Ruth Hill for her interview work. The original project was supported by the British Institute of Learning Disabilities and by Somerset Community Team for Adults with Learning Disabilities, and funded through the Big Lottery Fund and the Esmee Fairbairn Foundation. Openstorytellers is also grateful to Arts Council England for funding placements for storytellers with learning disabilities to develop skills in managing their company.

Notes

1 The Open College Network is one of the foremost accrediting bodies in the UK for adult education.
2 With his permission, I am using Robin's real name.
3 A well-known Irish legend (see www.ireland-information.com/articles/thechildrenoflir.htm).

References

Grove, N. (2004). It's my story. *Community Living, 17(3)*, 16–18.
Grove, N. (2009). *Learning to Tell.* BILD publications. Available at: www.bild.org.uk.
Johnson, L. (2009) How I create creativity (2): Defining who I am. *Speech and Language Therapy in Practice, November,* 26–28.
Kondrat, D. & Teater, B. (2009). An anti-stigma approach to working with persons with severe mental disability: Seeking real change through narrative change. *Journal of Social Work Practice, 23,* 35–47.
Labov, W. & Waletzky, J. (1976). Narrative analysis: Oral versions of personal experience. In J. Helm (Ed.), *Essays on the verbal and visual arts* (pp. 12–44). Seattle, WA: University of Washington Press.
Norrick, N. R. (2000). *Conversational narrative. Storytelling in everyday talk.* Amsterdam: John Benjamins.
Peterson, C., & McCabe, A. (1983). *Developmental psycholinguistics: Three ways of looking at a child's narrative.* New York: Plenum Press.
Renfrew, C. (1997). *Bus Story Test.* Milton Keynes: Speechmark. See also http://busstory.us for North American edition
Vygotsky, L. (1978). *Mind in society.* Cambridge, MA: Harvard University Press.
Walmsley, J. & Johnson, K. (2003). *Inclusive research with people with learning disabilities: past, present and future.* Gateshead: Athenaeum Press.

Chapter 9

Multi-sensory stories in story-packs

Chris Fuller

Background

This approach to storytelling was designed for children, young people and adults who are unlikely to be able to appreciate regular stories because of their profound intellectual and multiple disabilities (PIMD), and it requires the stories to be in a particular physical format. The pages are A3 laminated cards with sensory objects and materials attached, for the listener to handle, hear, smell, look at and feel as the story unfolds. It is known as the multisensory storytelling technique (MSST).

In a story-pack every action required to make the page 'work' must cater for any physical disability, so size, shape, space between the object and the card, and position on the card are all designed to be accessible and there is only one sensory experience per page. 'Look at' pages are clear, colourful, defined shapes which are glued to the page so that those with no sight or dual impairment can still feel them. Smells are absorbed into fabric or wafted from their original containers and can be pleasant but are also great fun if they are unpleasant! Materials for tactile pages need to be refreshingly different from everyday tactile experiences – sequinned fabric, wire netting, chains, artificial grass, a squashy ball, vibrating toys – and sounds can range from the soft whisper of a dog toy with the squeaker removed to a metal spoon banging on a frying pan!

Most objects will be mounted on or tied to a page card with a length of cord or elastic so that there is a 'field' against which it is used and the storyteller can control a listener's action if necessary. The large size of the card allows time for the brain to acknowledge what the hand is feeling and provides sufficient space for attaching a moving mechanism such as a gate bolt or a letterbox so that the listener can experience a variety of actions. One or two objects will need to be unattached – a plant spray, a towel, a funny wig!

The stories are short and for each brief block of text, usually just one sentence, there is an accompanying page card, and a sound or a smell will be introduced at the point where attention may lag. The storyline carries the emotion of the story through the storyteller's voice, as the listeners will not necessarily understand the words, and it invites exaggerated voice tones, pitch and volume to create phrases of sound which will gradually become memorable. In this way it eventually offers the opportunity for sentences and page cards to be anticipated, the joy of a familiar story often told. The whole story, generally seven to ten sentences, is in enlarged print on a single A3 laminated sheet and placed on the floor. This allows the storyteller to have both hands free to help the listener to use the page cards.

Principles and theory

Underpinning the practice is the fact that every sensation is a form of information which feeds the nervous system, and sensations come from every joint, muscle, area of skin and sense organ in the head to send sensory input to the brain. The senses which give us most of our conscious awareness of the world are sight, sound, touch and hearing (Ayres, 1982). We therefore have many pathways through which we can reach children and adults with profound developmental delay, and give them a sensation.

Research into access to literature (Webb, 1992 quoted in Grove, 2005) suggests that early response begins with a sensory experience that alerts us to what is there. Our feelings then assess the sensory experience and it is the bond between feeling and language that is the foundation of literature. Through our feelings, a story becomes a story and not just a list of events, and so the storyline must have a crescendo of happenings leading to a dramatic or significant middle. In tandem, the objects and materials in a multisensory story must also seek to generate appropriate feelings for the storyline; a bonfire can glow and crackle with red rustling plastic, a fairy laugh can be tinkling bells, the urgency of catching the school bus may be a loud horn!

So we now have relevant sensory input but what will enable the listener to focus on it? As children with PIMD have attention skills that are developmentally early, it is the joint attention and joint action which occur when storyteller and listener are using a page card or are engaged together in an action that support their ability to attend to their own actions (Charman et al., 2001).

Finally, we need to think about the delivery of the storyline. Research into early language development has found that babies need to hear multiple sound signals so that the brain neurons can map the sounds and look for consistencies. At this stage the brain is not concentrating on what the words mean but on segmenting the speech sounds and looking for consistencies (Tallal, 2004). We also tend to exaggerate our voice when speaking to a baby: 'Oh look at YOU!', which amplifies and enhances the acoustic information. The same research revealed that children with language delay have a slower auditory processing threshold. For listeners in the early stage of language development or on the autistic spectrum, repeating a story many times and using an exaggerated and slower style of delivery will give them the best possible chance of being alert to a phrase of sound and eventually learning it.

Any story can be delivered in this way – fictional, factual, traditional, personal – but the content and concepts of the stories need to be pared down to a limited number of short sentences and the end of a sentence should reflect the action to be taken on its corresponding page card. There are ready-made story-packs available (Bag Books; see 'Where to go'), but anyone can make their own to deliver virtually any subject in the curriculum or purely for pleasure, designed with contents and storyline specifically for the chronological age of the listener(s).

History

My own approach to multisensory storytelling began in 1989, when a group of six 4 to 6-year-olds with PIMD had been placed after lunch in a semicircle at one end of their classroom and looked just like any infant class waiting for a story.

On the shelf lay a box of 'tactile cards' made to encourage the pupils to look, listen, feel, reach for and grasp. Taking one with flapping bottle tops, another with crinkled silver survival blanket, a third covered in bubble wrap and a fourth with a piece of nylon net over rustling polystyrene packing pieces, I told a simple story about a bookseller who travelled from house to house with his donkey (the bottle tops). He invited each child to feel the three pages of his 'book' but no one had any money to buy, so they asked him to try their friend next door and were then helped to touch the person next to them. The child who was last in the line had a bag of money – the class money for drinks! She bought it, and together we emptied the money into a shiny tin, which was then rattled vigorously around the group for fun.

The children appeared to empathise with the story, the cards were 'spot on' for their interest value, everyone was actively involved in feeling each 'page', their turn came quickly and when the donkey sound flapped around the group it continually refreshed their attention. I wrote the story down so that it could be retold exactly the same, and repeated it every day. During the following weeks the children's enjoyment appeared to grow.

The success of this first story inspired a 'do-it-yourself' manual containing six stories and how to construct the corresponding multisensory story-packs (Fuller, 1990).

Work in practice

In a typical session the storyteller sits opposite or close beside a single listener, but stands in front of a group, to help them to use the page card or make the action, and also to respond immediately to any reaction – an eye blink, involuntary gesture, change of facial expression or body position, or the smallest sound.

Everyone sits on a chair, wheelchair or raised equipment such as a side-lyer, arranged in a semicircle with the ends curving inwards and with their accompanying staff or carers sitting behind them. Listeners with challenging behaviour sit at either end with their support member beside them. This seating has several advantages. The page cards can travel uninterrupted from one listener to the next as the short piece of text is repeated, the pages are roughly at the same level and the curved seating gives everyone the opportunity to be aware of each other's reactions. Having a stable base helps listeners to focus their attention and stay in the group, and the storyteller can oversee the whole group at a glance.

When the storyteller is unfamiliar with the group, they introduce themselves by shaking each person's hand and this reveals the listeners' dominant hand. For someone who is tactile defensive, their hand is taken very briefly to feel or use the page contents and then released immediately. If this continues to be intolerable, each card is placed on their lap or activated by their foot or another body part. For a hand that needs time and help to unclench, the sentence is repeated until their grasp is successful and comfortable.

The sentences are said slowly and clearly for each listener, with pauses, pitch, tone and volume exaggerated to create that memorable phrase of sound and to engage the listeners in the emotional feel of the story: happy, funny, crazy, scary, charming etc. Then the listeners 'tell' the story through their actions and at the end the storyteller will praise them: 'Give yourselves a clap, you're brilliant!', which is also the clue that the story is finished.

Outcomes and evidence: What we look for

Every listener accesses and enjoys the stories at their own developmental level, which means that the stories can be used with a group of mixed intellectual ability. Outcomes can begin at the most basic stage, that of the listeners purely being exposed to the stories' range and variety of linguistic, physical, and emotional experiences, being able to tolerate the required physical interaction and displaying simple reflex responses. For someone with no voluntary movement, progress will be muscles relaxed and ready to make the aided movement for a familiar page, and increased attention skills. Others will learn to reach and grasp and in due course to make the action unaided. Some people will smile at the familiar phrases, others will look and enjoy their peers' reactions, and some listeners will be able to repeat or remember certain phrases and eventually be able to tell the story themselves.

When a story has been repeated many times there is evidence of increased alertness and anticipation, improved attention skills and real pleasure in hearing the expected (Fuller, 1991), and in factual personal stories, proof that a sequence has been learnt (Watson, Lambe & Hogg, 2002; Fenwick, 2005, 2007; Young et al., 2011). Progress is assessed by using video and regular recording on observation sheets that monitor focus of attention, attention span, anticipation, communication skills, social interaction, interaction with pages, behaviours indicating enjoyment or displeasure and for more able listeners, comprehension and acquired vocabulary.

The story of Freddie

An example of one small person's progress is 5-year-old Freddie who, when he first came to his new special school, was scared of virtually everything. Developmentally around 18 months and tiny for his age, he would bottom shuffle his way into a corner of the classroom and screech if another pupil came near him. He never touched anything with his hands and kept his gaze down.

In his first term I told a multisensory story called *Desmond* three times a week, and as soon as he saw the story-pack box he would move himself round sideways on his chair and turn his head away. When it came to his turn I rested each page card on his knee and he would squirm further round in his chair to get away from it. Then one day I noticed that after the page had left him he looked up and watched the other children using it. By the third week he was smiling at the cat sound when the other pupils laughed, but still facing sideways and hiding when it was his turn.

He needed help to be brave and join in, and so the following week I took his left hand and rested it on the nylon cat fur page and we stroked downwards just once. The hand shot back out of my grasp but he turned his face forward for the cat sound and laughed. It took only two more weeks before Freddie could sit straight in his chair and would allow his hand to be taken to use every page. By the end of the half term he could do it himself and would flap his hands excitedly when the first page came out of the box. At first a new story-pack would mean his reverting to hiding until he was familiar with it by watching the others, but eventually a new story was exciting.

Working with adults

Working with adults has also been interesting. By exercising their right to choose not to engage in an activity, some people have become so withdrawn from contact that it has become a habit. During a training workshop for day-centre staff, I took the hand of one young man to help him use a page card and there was a sharp intake of breath from his assistant: 'Oh he's tactile defensive, we always do it for him.' He did withdraw his hand immediately afterwards but had not actively resisted that touch. In fact I was able to help him use every page of the following four stories and, by the end, his hand was still up by his ear but relaxed and ready to move down. He was enjoying being involved and so was receptive to the stories, the language and the fun.

Whilst teaching in special schools I used MSST for 9 years before establishing and heading Bag Books, a publisher of hand-crafted multisensory stories. During that time it became clear that 'having something to do', interacting with a member of staff who is repeating short dynamic pieces of text, and is physically close, enabled my pupils with severe and profound intellectual difficulties to focus their attention and be happily engaged throughout a 30 minute story session. The evidence available from research into developing literacy though multisensory storytelling in children with PIMD (Watson et al., 2002) indicates that the benefits are due to all the components of the stories, from the social context to the reinforcing stimuli, to the appropriate language. 'The packs do indeed hold the listener's attention and connect with the child in a meaningful and enjoyable way' (Hogg, 2004) and this is in accord with Bag Books' own monitoring across all ages.

Contexts of learning

Although originally devised for children and adults with PIMD, multisensory storytelling is an inclusive resource for listeners who have a range of different difficulties. These include young children with mild learning difficulties (MLD); children on the autistic spectrum; those with attention deficit hyperactivity disorder (ADHD); children and older people with severe learning difficulties (SLD); young children who have visual impairment or no sight, or are both hearing and vision impaired, and mainstream 3 to 6-year-olds who are just not used to sitting still. This makes it ideal for a family or care home, a mainstream inclusive nursery, the special school classroom, library story times and adult services for people with profound and severe intellectual disabilities.

Multisensory story-packs have also been used extensively with young children who have English as a second language. Initially they do not need to understand the story in order to take part, but gradually the short sentences help them to learn words and phrases. As part of good integration practice, story-packs can also be designed around the beliefs and practices of other cultures, with storylines which reflect the everyday life of different communities and include culturally appropriate artefacts.

Try it yourself

Top tips

- Familiarise yourself thoroughly with the page cards and storyline before you start and take time to arrange the listeners and support staff/carers.
- Say the sentences exactly as they are written, so that the phrase of sound remains consistent.
- Be energetic in the delivery so that the listeners are caught up in your enthusiasm.

Where to go

Training and a training DVD are available from Bag Books, and many libraries across the UK have received training and stock story-packs (www.bagbooks.org). The organisation PAMIS, in Scotland, is also a veteran of multisensory storytelling. To make a start, however, borrow a story-pack from a library, learn and practise it at home and then persuade a friend or family member to let you take their hand and try it out with them.

Websites and resources

Bag Books: www.bagbooks.org
PAMIS: www.pamis.org.uk

References

Ayres, J. A. (1982). *Sensory integration and the child*. Torrance, CA: Western Psychological Services.

Charman, T., Baron-Cohen, S., Swettenham, J., Baird, G., Cox, A. & Drew, A. (2001). Testing joint attention, imitation and play as infancy precursors to language and theory of mind. *Cognitive Development, 15(4)*, 481–485.

Fenwick, M. (2005). Multisensory sensitive stories. *Eye Contact: RNIB, 42*, 12–14.

Fenwick, M. (2007). Sensitive stories. *Insight: RNIB, 10*, 30–32.

Fuller, C. (1990). *Tactile stories: A do-it-yourself manual*. London: Bag Books.

Fuller, C. (1991). *Tactile stories: Training DVD*. London: Bag Books.

Grove, N. (2005). *Ways into literature* London: David Fulton.

Hogg, J. (2004). *Bag Books Annual Review*. London: Bag Books.

Tallal, P. (2004). Improving language and literacy is a matter of time. *Neuroscience, 5*, 721–728.

Watson, M., Lambe, L. & Hogg, J. (2002). *Real lives: Real stories*. Dundee:
University of Dundee: PAMIS.

Webb, E. (1992). *Literature in education: Encounter and experience*. London: Falmer Press.

Young, H.B., Fenwick, M., Lambe, L. & Hogg, J. (2011). Multi-sensory storytelling as an aid to assisting people with profound intellectual disabilities to cope with sensitive issues: a multiple research methods analysis of engagement and outcomes. *European Journal of Special Needs Education, 26*, 127–142.

Chapter 10

Storytelling with all our senses
mehr-Sinn® Geschichten

Barbara Fornefeld
Translation by Ingeborg Sungen

> As soon as Lena is lying in her hammock and notices how I open the story-box, her face starts beaming. She knows that we are going to start our journey to Treasure Island.
>
> (Maike Schnitzler)

Background

mehr-Sinn® Geschichten (multisensory stories) are stories which are not simply told but can be experienced with all our senses. They are stories to look at, listen to, smell and taste, to feel and to experience. They have their own way to be told and they are stored in story-boxes. Since they can be experienced by multiple senses and can be characterised by a simple but expressive language and inspiring music to evoke atmospheres and emotions, multisensory stories have developed into recreational options for families and educational options for institutions for people with profound intellectual and multiple disabilities (PIMD) and homes for elderly people.

Although mehr-Sinn® Geschichten were originally developed for children, adolescents and adults with profound and multiple disabilities, they can also give pleasure to people without any disabilities. They aim to eliminate the prejudice that people with profound disabilities are unable to understand fairy tales and other stories. Additionally, they aim to enable them to experience cultural participation.

mehr-Sinn® Geschichten have been developed in a common project between Cologne University and the association KuBus®.[1] Professionally supported students retell the contents of fairy tales,[2] myths,[3] legends[4] or tales from the Bible[5] and prepare educational versions. They elaborate non-fiction stories[6] with corresponding materials and put them into practice with people with PIMD. Subsequently, KuBus starts to distribute them (see Figure 10.1).

Nice wooden boxes store sensory materials like soft rag dolls, glittering bowls, small boxes with odorous spices and many other inspiring things. The materials have been developed and compiled in cooperation with an institution for people with PIMD in Saarbrucken, Germany. All story-boxes contain a CD with appropriate music and sounds that have been specifically composed and recorded for each multisensory story by Hans Steinmeier, composer, arranger and director of the North-Rhine Westphalian Federal Police Orchestra, and his co-musicians. The story-boxes are also equipped with director's booklets including the narrative texts and special hints for how to present and narrate the story, supported by its materials, in an easily understandable way. In the case of a fairy tale, a print of the original version is included. A handbook gives information about the development and the method of multisensory storytelling.

Figure 10.1 The *Little Red Riding Hood* box.

The underlying idea is that multisensory storytelling always addresses the person as a whole and not only her or his cognitive abilities. The sound of the narrator's voice, her or his activities, the sensory materials and the music awaken emotions and create images. In experiencing through their different senses, comprehension is made possible for people with profound disabilities.

Principles

The concept of multisensory storytelling combines elements of the storytelling method with the old tradition of narrating fairy tales. It systematically explores fairy tales, myths and legends from the German heritage – and that of everyone.

Fairy tales originate from a time when only few people were able to read and very few possessed books. It was an oral time, when stories were orally passed on from one generation to the next and were cultivated by all social classes. At that time storytelling was a means to relax, flee from everyday life and accompany the transition from waking to sleeping (cp. Wittenhorst, 2010, p. 28ff). These customs survived today.

In the eighteenth century, the brothers Jacob and William Grimm collected national myths and fairy tales in order to explore them scientifically, a work which has met with great approval in many countries. Today, the 'brothers Grimm' are known as the founders of German philology and their collection of fairy tales has become famous all over the world.

Fairy tales, myths, legends and other genres of narration represent a part of our culture that accompanies us while we are growing up. Who does not like to remember her or his childhood, being read to aloud at bedtime, or other situations when stories carried us off into extraordinary, cosy or remote atmospheres? We were not always able to understand every word immediately, but we always experienced the tension or the wit of the story and always felt touched by it. Most of us keep these narrative moments, with their special interpersonal relationships, as good memories.

Stories and fairy tales touch us in a special way and lead us to 'the things themselves', to our fundamental experiences and emotions like fear, grief, hope or pride. They relate to basic needs of mankind, like appreciation or security. They concern 'man as she/he really is' (cp. Lüthi, 2004.).

People with profound disabilities have fundamental experiences and needs. They have lived through fear, grief, hope, pride or defiance, and they long for security and appreciation. Parents, who are often closer to their children's emotions than others, are able to recognise these experiences and needs. But carers in institutions for people with PIMD, who usually express themselves only in spoken language, sometimes cannot imagine that understanding without language is also possible. People with profound disabilities express their understanding of the world by means of changes in behaviour. Carers who have not learned to look at such changes or to listen to them tend to miss these behavioural expressions and the basic experiences and needs of people with PIMD. Carers might also think that stories are simply told by means of spoken words and can only be understood on a rational level. But the narrator's voice, the prosody of her or his language, and the special atmosphere also help people to understand a story. Barbara Senckel (2002), who researched the effects of fairy tales on people with profound disabilities, draws the conclusion that they are an appropriate genre of literature for these children and adults. Fairy tales not only represent a common cultural heritage where people with and without disabilities can meet each other, but also open up opportunities for them both to develop their personalities.

People with PIMD are able to understand the content of stories if they are told in a way they are able to understand. The concept of mehr-Sinn® Geschichten is based on cultural studies and educational science, and its method of multisensory storytelling is based on an educational theory. The story-boxes with their sensory materials stimulate aesthetic experiences that make it easier to understand the story as a whole. This was expressed by a carer in a workshop for people with PIMD, who was asked about the listeners' reactions on the storytelling: 'They were curious, interested, some were very alert. You could see their joy, tension and pleasure. The target to experience the story by multiple senses has been achieved.'

This statement shows that stories can be understood on a pre-narrative[7] or pre-verbal level, an aspect which up to now has been insufficiently explored by special education. Stories address people in a special way that refers to the person as a whole. They help to generate identity and bring people closer to each other.

History

mehr-Sinn® Geschichten are inspired by Nicola Grove's *Ways into Literature* (2005) as well as by Loretto Lambe and James Hogg's multisensory storytelling (Lambe & Hogg, 2011). They also go back to Chris Fuller's idea of 'Bag Books' (Fuller, 1999) and her method of telling a story in a simple way. However, mehr-Sinn® Geschichten differ from the approach of multisensory storytelling with regard to their theoretical principles, their intentions, the aesthetic composition of the story-boxes and materials, and the method of storytelling.

The educational concept of mehr-Sinn® Geschichten results from a long-term scientific discussion about the education of people with PIMD. It started in the 1980s with practical experiences in the education of pupils with profound disabilities and with the effort to provide them with cultural and educational content. The discussion of a sense-oriented pedagogy by Langeveld and Danner (1981), of a phenomenology of perception by Merleau-Ponty (1966)[8] and an aesthetic experience by Waldenfels (2010) and Wiesing (2009) led to a pedagogic concept for people with PIMD by Fornefeld (1989, 1991, 2001), which concentrates on the philosophy of the 'Leib' and postulates the comprehension and experience of cultural opportunities which are perceptible to the senses. Multisensory storytelling assumes that narrators and listeners share common experiences. The process of storytelling initiates a dialogue between both, which is based on intercorporeality[9] (cp. Fornefeld, 2009). This dialogue proves the importance of literacy experiences (cp. Gross-Kunkel, 2011), which help people with PIMD to understand the main plot of a literary text if it is edited and condensed to its essential elements (cp. Heinen, 2003).

Work in practice

Each mehr-Sinn® Geschichte is stored in an individually equipped wooden box. 'The story-boxes are designed in such an inspiring way. You do not have to look for materials. Everything is immediately at hand,' reported a speech therapist who was testing mehr-Sinn® Geschichten in her practice at an early stage of development of our project. One student who cares for an old lady in a seniors' home relates that the old lady always asks her: 'You've got a box with you, don't you?' She particularly likes the fairy tale of *Little Red Riding Hood* because it reminds her of her childhood.

mehr-Sinn® Geschichten are not only suitable for people with profound disabilities but for everybody, because they turn the process of storytelling into an extraordinary experience. Each story is printed in a shorter and a longer version so that it can be adapted to the listener's level of comprehension. For fairy tales like *Hansel and Gretel* or legends like *The Little People of Cologne* there is an extra print of the original version included. 'Due to the different versions of the story, the music and the materials all children of a group can benefit from the storytelling process,' a kindergarten worker said after she tried a mehr-Sinn® Geschichte with her heterogeneous group and after all children enthusiastically joined in. This shows that mehr-Sinn® Geschichten are inclusive, too.

Interviews with carers who have been working with mehr-Sinn® Geschichten in different institutions for people with PIMD prove that these people can benefit from these experiences. A remedial teacher working with a group of adults with profound disabilities said:

> First our residents were irritated when I put the story-box with *The Oriental Market* on the table. But after I had told the story once, they wanted to listen to it again and again and refused to stop. All were very attentive, even those I would have never expected it from. It gives me so much pleasure to tell stories in such a way.

Another carer told the mehr-Sinn® Geschichte *Hansel and Gretel* (according to the brothers Grimm) to children with PIMD and summarised: 'The children have come closer to me.' Video recordings of single case studies about multisensory storytelling have revealed that people with PIMD listen to the stories, turn towards the narrators, and react by their behaviour.

The story of Jens

In a school for blind children, Britta Sommer, a student, chose the religious mehr-Sinn® Geschichte *Jesus and the Storm* to work with 7-year-old Jens. This boy has profound intellectual impairments; he is blind and was born with tetraplegia. While his classmates were being taught he was just present in the room. Mrs Sommer was deeply convinced that Jens could understand something if he was offered appropriate subject matter. Therefore she developed the religious story *Jesus and the Storm* for him. Jens showed by his body tension and smacking sounds that he always enjoyed it when she entered the class. He liked the story and wanted to listen to it again and again. Mrs Sommer commented on his reactions: 'It is my personal desire to create other multisensory story-boxes in order to let pupils with profound disabilities participate in religious education.' To tell and to listen to stories connects people with each other. It connects adults with children, and people with and without profound disabilities. Storytelling has a social impact because it builds bridges between people.

Development of mehr-Sinn® Geschichten

In order to achieve the aim of promoting understanding, mehr-Sinn® Geschichten require a process of multidimensional development and analysis (Figure 10.2), which normally takes six months and tries to answer the following two questions:

1   At the beginning there is the story, the literary original or the so-called 'what', which undergoes a scientific and didactic analysis according to linguistic and educational classification, structure of language and contents, and educational implementation.
2   The question of 'how' to transmit the content and 'how' to dramatise the narration should be answered as follows:
    a   The plot should be told in precise words and simple sentences.
    b   The dramatisation of the story should also consider the decision on 'with what' and refer to all sensory materials and music.
    c   With regard to 'who' is involved, mehr-Sinn® Geschichten differentiate between two target persons, the listener and the narrator. Narrating and listening are closely linked to each other and have to be carefully harmonised.
    d   Next is the 'where'. An appropriate atmosphere of narration is important for the sensory–aesthetic process of comprehension, which means that we need to specify the appropriate time and place.
    e   The 'what for', which is the aim of achieving cultural and social participation, also has to be considered in relation to dramatisation, materials, situation and contents.

When developing mehr-Sinn® Geschichten, special emphasis has to be put on the prosody of language and the quality of music because both support the process of sensory–aesthetic comprehension (cp. Brandstätter, 2008, Lampson, 2010).

Outcomes and evidence: What we look for

Once the process of developing a mehr-Sinn® Geschichte is finished, the quality of the story has to be tested in single case studies with regard to content, dramatisation, materials and music. Video analyses are carried out by means of criteria-based behaviour observations

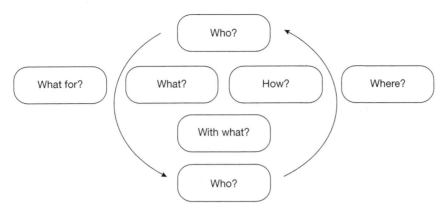

Figure 10.2 The multidimensional development of mehr-sinn® Geschichten.

(Schnitzler, 2008; Lehmann, 2009; Wittenhorst, 2010; Schulte, 2011; Sommer, 2011; Naumann, 2011). Between September 2010 and January 2011 six new mehr-Sinn® Geschichten were tested in 25 institutions such as families, kindergartens, special schools for mentally disabled, physically disabled or blind people, homes for elderly people and homes for people with PIMD. All participants showed distinct reactions of attention, such as changed breathing frequency, a turn of the head, a smile or a vocalisation, when they were listening to the story for the first time. These reactions became even more distinctive, and the participants showed by their behaviour which parts of the story, which sensory materials and which music especially touched them. In all cases the listeners' behaviour corresponded to the special atmosphere.

The quality of the stories was evaluated by means of semi-structured questionnaires and narrative interviews. All feedback was positive, the innovative character of the concept was emphasised and its practicality was approved. Suggestions by the institutions were integrated into our concept; for example, longer versions of the texts for listeners with greater speech comprehension. So we developed a second plot, concerning logic and language, which fits into the first one. This new version now enables us to tell the new stories in mixed groups.

Since the method of multisensory storytelling is new to many people, we were asked to develop an educational programme which addresses parents, carers and students. This programme is based on three key aspects:

1 Getting to know the concept of mehr-Sinn® Geschichten.
2 Experiencing by one's own senses as a basis to understand and interact.
3 Getting to know and experiencing the basic methods of mehr-Sinn® Geschichten.

Although many people are working with mehr-Sinn® Geschichten in various ways, the project is still a work in progress, and new stories are continuously being developed at Cologne University. In order to broaden the concept, we are watching what others do with the stories, listening to their experiences and paying attention to how people with profound disabilities react. Since all people involved are attentively listening to each other, all are establishing closer inter-relationships – listeners, storytellers and researchers.

Notes

1   The Association to Promote Culture, Education and Social Participation for People with and without Disabilities.
2   For example, *Hansel and Gretel* or *Little Red Riding Hood*, after the brothers Grimm.
3   For example, *The Myth of the Giant Mils.*
4   For example, *The Little People from Cologne*, after August Kopisch.
5   *Jesus and the Storm* (Sommer, 2011).
6   *A Walk in the Wood* or *The Boxing Match.*
7   Pre-narrative refers to a philosophical dimension of interpretation.
8   The concept of mehr-Sinn® Geschichten is based on, among others, the *Phenomenology of Perception* (1945) by Maurice Merleau-Ponty. He defines phenomenology as the study of essences, including the essence of perception and of consciousness. He also says, however, that phenomenology is a method of describing the nature of our perceptual contact with the world. Phenomenology is concerned with providing a direct description of human experience. Perception is the background of experience which guides every conscious action.
9   A fundamental dialogue between people; their responsivity.

References

Brandstätter, U. (2008). *Grundfragen der Ästhetik. Bild – Musik – Sprache – Körper.* Köln, Weimar, Wien: Böhlau UTB.

Fornefeld, B. (1991). 'Wahr-nehmen' und 'Sinn-stiften' des (behinderten) Menschen. Anthropologisch-pädagogische Aspekte kindlicher Erkenntnisgewinnung. *Behinderte in Familie, Schule und Gesellschaft, 14(3)*, 25–33.

Fornefeld, B. (1997). *Elementare Beziehung und Selbstverwirklichung geistig Schwerstbehinderter in sozialer Integration. Reflexionen im Vorfeld einer leiborientierten Pädagogik* (3rd ed.). PhD dissertation: University of Cologne. Aachen: Mainz Verlag.

Fornefeld, B. (2001). 'Wahr-nehmen' und 'Sinn-stiften' des behinderten Menschen. In K. Rühl & A. Längle (Eds), *Ich kann nicht . . . Behinderung als menschliches Phänomen* (pp. 27–39). Wien: WUV-Universitätsverlag.

Fornefeld, B. (2009). Bei Leibe gebildet – Sonderpädagogische Impulse. In *Zeitschrift für Heilpädagogik, 60(3)*, 107–114.

Fuller, C. (1999). Bag Books Tactile Stories. *The SLD Experience, 23*, 20–21.

Groß-Kunkel, A. (2011). Literacy-Erlebnisse für Menschen mit und ohne Behinderung. Soziale Teilhabe durch gemeinsames Lesen. In B. Fornefeld (Ed.), *Mehr-sinnliches Geschichtenerzählen: Eine Idee setzt sich durch* [Multi-sensory storytelling: An idea gets through]. Berlin, Münster, London: Lit Verlag.

Grove, N. (2005). *Ways into literature.* London: David Fulton.

Heinen, N. (2003). Überlegungen zur Didaktik mit Menschen mit schwerer Behinderung: Eine Zwischenbilanz. In Schulentwicklung. Gestaltungs(t)räume in der Arbeit mit schwerstbehinderten Schülerinnen und Schülern. In A. Fröhlich, W. Lamers & N. Heinen (Eds.), *Texte zur Körper- und Mehrfachbehindertenpädagogik* (pp. 121–143). Düsseldorf: Verlag Selbstbestimmtes Leben.

Lambe, L. & Hogg. J. (2011). Multi-sensory storytelling: PAMIS' practice, experience and research findings. In Fornefeld, B. (Ed.), *Mehr-sinnliches Geschichtenerzählen: Eine Idee setzt sich durch* [Multi-sensory Storytelling: An idea gets through] (pp. 15–40). Berlin, Münster, London: Lit Verlag.

Lampson, E. (2010). Spiegelungen der Stille: Zwischen Hören und Denken. *Journal Phänomenologie, 33*, 20–26.

Langeveld, M. J. & Danner, H. (1981). *Methodologie und Sinn-Orientierung in der Pädagogik.* München: Ernst Reinhardt.

Lehmann, K. (2009). *mehr-Sinn® Geschichten. Ein Mehr an kultureller Teilhabe für Menschen mit schwerer Behinderung.* Examination paper: Universität zu Köln.

Lüthi, M. (2004). *Märchen* (10th ed.). Stuttgart/Weimar: Metzler Verlag.

Merleau-Ponty, M. (1966). *Phänomenologie der Wahrnehmung.* Berlin: Walter de Gruyter.

Naumann, M. (2011). *Freizeitpädagogik für Menschen mit Komplexer Behinderung? Mehr-sinnliches Geschichtenerzählen: Ein anwendungsbezogenes Schulungskonzept.* Diploma thesis: Universität zu Köln.

Schnitzler, M. (2008). *Kulturelle Lebenswelten für Schüler mit schwerer Behinderung. Eine mehr-Sinn® Geschichte für Lea.* Examination paper: Universität zu Köln.

Schulte, I. P. (2011). *Bildung mit mehr-Sinn®: Responsivität und Bildung.* Examination paper: Universität zu Köln.

Senckel, B. (2002). 'In den alten Zeiten, wo das Wünschen noch geholfen hat . . .' Märchenstrukturen und die Struktur präoperativen Denkens. *Geistige Behinderung, 41(2),* 115–125.

Sommer, B. (2011). *'Jesus und der Sturm': mehr-Sinn® Geschichten als religiöse Teilhabe für Menschen mit schwerer Behinderung.* Examination paper: Universität zu Köln.

Waldenfels, B. (2010). *Sinne und Künste im Wechselspiel. Modi ästhetischer Erfahrung.* Frankfurt a.M.: Suhrkamp Verlag.

Wiesing, L. (2009). *Das Mich der Wahrnehmung: Eine Autopsie.* Frankfurt a.M.: Suhrkamp Verlag.

Wittenhorst, M. (2010). *Geschichtenerzählen einmal anders: Märchen erleben durch mehr-sinnliches Geschichtenerzählen.* Examination paper: Universität zu Köln.

Chapter 11

Sensitive stories

Tackling challenges for people with profound intellectual disabilities through multisensory storytelling

Loretto Lambe and James Hogg

Background

The development of multisensory storytelling took as its starting point the expressed need in the late 1990s of family carers, teachers and other professionals for the development of a holistic context which would provide an enjoyable and meaningful activity with developmental significance for people with profound intellectual and multiple disabilities (PIMD). *PAMIS* responded to this demand by developing the work of Chris Fuller at Bag Books (Fuller, 1990, 1999 and see Chapter 9) through the creation of individualised, personal stories. By individualisation we mean not only a narrative of personal significance but also a choice of materials that are appropriate in terms of age, sensory characteristics and relevant interactions.

The stories were initially developed to promote learning in the context of a personal story (Watson et al., 2002). Subsequently they evolved to provide a means for parents and teachers to engage individuals with PIMD with topics that presented difficulties for them with respect, for example, to sexual development, transitions or health interventions (Fenwick, 2005, 2007; Young et al., 2010).

The approach is particularly aimed at children and adults who have profound and multiple learning disabilities; that is, they have complex health needs, sensory impairments and great difficulty in communicating, in addition to profound intellectual disabilities (Hogg, et al., 2007; Nakken & Vlaskamp, 2002). The starting point is the development of a narrative relevant specifically, but not necessarily exclusively, to a given individual. This begins with the identification of events and experiences of importance to the person, as reported and developed by those most familiar with him or her, typically a parent and/or professional. This narrative consists of a set of events that are linked either causally or temporally in a connected sequence. Typically the narrative reflects and exemplifies real-world experiences. We view storytelling as the sequence of communicative acts conveying the narrative through interactive, multisensory presentation. It is important that each of these interactions should be seen as part of the whole and related to the overall meaning of the narrative.

Theories

The theoretical basis of multisensory storytelling takes as its starting point the difficulties that affect people with PIMD, which include:

Communicative difficulties   These result in the failure of other individuals to respond contingently and consistently to communicative approaches. This results in a breakdown of interaction, which may be abbreviated and inconsistent (Grove et al., 1999).

In relation to these difficulties, the activity of storytelling provides a single context in which the storyteller and individual with PIMD may interact with their joint focus on the story media; careful structuring of the story within a defined timeframe permits the storyteller to pace contingent responses and, where necessary, intervene to facilitate interactions with the material.

Sensory impairment Although difficult to assess, impairments of vision and hearing are undoubtedly highly prevalent (Evenhuis et al., 2001), restricting what may be experienced in the natural environment.

The development of multisensory stories permits careful choice of the stimulus material. Impairments are taken into account either by increased emphasis on the senses that are available or through accentuating the intensity of stimuli in the impaired modality.

Personhood In people with PIMD, personhood is viewed as the outcome of social interaction and the meaning of individuals to each other (Hogg, 2011; Kittay, 2011), including the acknowledgement of the meaningfulness of the life of the person.

At the core of the creation of the present multisensory stories is the acknowledgment of the individual as a person with interests and concerns unique to her or his life. The telling of the story involves a period in which the personhood of that individual is the focus of joint attention without other distractions.

Learning It has been widely accepted for the past three decades that individuals with PIMD have the capacity to learn, given appropriate interventions, though the conditions under which learning does occur are often not available (Hogg & Sebba, 1986a, 1986b).

Learning is an inherent part of the activity and the approach provides the opportunity to set clear learning outcomes through repeated sessions that ensure consistent practice and feedback.

Mood and motivation Recent years have seen the acknowledgement that people with PIMD experience changing mood and motivation (Ross & Oliver, 2003). There is also agreement that learning will take place most effectively when a person is enjoying an activity and motivated to engage in it (Miller, 2003).

The motivational potential of multisensory storytelling arises because it is inherently enjoyable for both listener and storyteller, making engagement (as an outcome of motivation to participate) an intrinsic part of the activity. However, such enjoyment can be an end in itself and use of the stories as a leisure activity is as legitimate as other outcome-focused uses.

Principles

The guiding principles cover the creation of the story, its production as a physical entity and the way in which it is told.

Creating the multisensory story

All stories are personal to the intended listener. Each story was developed through collab-oration between the parent, the teacher (or other professional), and a member of *PAMIS* staff whose role it was co-ordinate the activity. Where relevant, a specialist in the subject of the story contributed; for example, a community dentist for visits to the dentist or a learning disability epilepsy nurse for epilepsy; a community nurse specialising in sexual health gave advice regarding stories concerned with sexual development and activity. Each draft of the narrative was reviewed and developed by the team involved, who also determined the sensory stimuli to be used (which would initially be piloted with the individual). The physical production of the story was undertaken in-house by *PAMIS* staff.

The story book

The book cover is a cardboard box containing the pages of the story with the sensory objects, and the storyline written on a single laminated sheet. The box is easy to transport when the story is lent to a family or school. It also gives a clear indication to the person with PIMD that the story is about to be told, emphasised by a visual and tactile stimulus on the 'spine' of the box.

There are between six and eight laminated A3 board pages in a story. The sensory stimuli are attached to each board, which is neutral in colour, typically one object per page. The objects are personal to the particular listener, appropriate to their age and stage of develop-ment, and convey the key concept in that phase of the narrative.

One or two short and well-rounded sentences associated with each page, to be used by the storyteller, are written on a matt laminated story card. The words relate directly to the sensory stimuli, are age appropriate and intended to be comprehensible for that individual and to others with similar needs.

Although the stories developed in the *PAMIS* 'Real Lives: Real Stories' project were created for specific individuals, the intention was that they could be enjoyed by others with PIMD. In practice this certainly proved to be the case, with a high and steady flow of requests for loans throughout Scotland. Full details, with illustrations of the material, are presented in Lambe and Hogg (2011). Figure 11.1 shows the components of a *PAMIS* multisensory story.

Telling the story

In the work undertaken by *PAMIS*, the same storyteller is involved for each individual throughout the scheduled readings. However, in 'free' use of the stories, when they are lent out, they may be told by a number of people. Consistency can be ensured by following the guidance printed on the reverse of the storyline card. This includes advice to:

- Ensure that presentation of each page is in the person's field of vision and reach.
- Use the voice expressively, with varied intonation, pitch and volume.
- Speak slowly and use pauses, enabling the person to process what she or he is hearing.
- Convey the atmosphere of the story.
- Ensure consistency in telling, without deviation or improvisation, which also means that the story can be told in a relatively short time, optimising the listener's attention.
- Present the pages and sensory material in a way which makes them accessible for the listener.

Figure 11.1 The components of a *PAMIS* multisensory story.

Outcomes and evidence: What we look for

The evaluation of multisensory storytelling as an aid to learning and coping with difficult experiences has employed multimethod research techniques, involving both interviews with participants and behavioural analysis of videoed sessions – typically of the first storytelling session, a middle session and the final session – although in reality the storytellers often continued with the story after the formal research frame (for details see Brewer & Hunter, 2006; Watson et al., 2002; Young et al., 2011). Behaviours were coded using microanalytical techniques with Observer Video-Pro® software (Noldus et al., 2000). These computerised recordings allowed us to look at a range of representations; for example, graphing the relationship in time between page presentation and withdrawal, key behaviours related to engagement with the story and storyteller, and learning objectives. The recorded observations could then be summarised in various ways and graphed appropriately. Figure 11.2, for example, shows (A) an increase in both looking at and touching the stimulus objects, and (B) the simultaneous reduction in visual social engagement with the storyteller.

Parents and professionals were interviewed at the end of the project. Questions dealt with their experience of the use of multisensory storytelling and how effective it had been in enabling their son or daughter to cope with the sensitive issue (i.e. whether the intended outcome had been achieved). Their responses during the telling of the story were also explored. Full details of the research methods and findings are provided by Young, Fenwick, Lambe and Hogg (2011).

Further research outwith the context of *PAMIS* work has been undertaken and has explored a number of issues, including staff interactive style during multisensory storytelling (Penne et al., 2012; Maes & Petry, 2006), meaningfulness to carers (Penne & Maes, 2011)

Joseph – Engagement with story

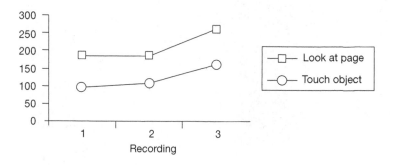

Joseph – Social engagement

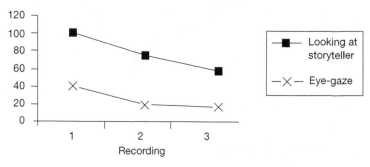

Figure 11.2 An example of data derived from the computerised analysis.

and the consistency with which *PAMIS* guidelines were followed (ten Brug et al., 2012; Vlaskamp et al., 2011). It is important to emphasise that future research will need to consider the issue of consistency in delivery of the stories if findings are to be compared and general lessons learnt.

In the 'Real Lives: Real Stories' project there were agreed learning targets built in that were linked to the person's individual educational programme (IEP) at school. Additionally, a target or concept that the parent wanted was also included. The teachers involved in the project all reported that the stories fitted well into the curriculum and the pupils' IEPs. Learning targets were achieved and, most importantly, the individual pupil and her or his classmates enjoyed having the story read again and again. Parents reported that the stories gave them another activity they could do with their daughter or son with PIMD, an activity that was both enjoyable and provided a means of helping them to understand concepts and situations.

The story of Craig

Craig was 14 years old at the time of the study. He had PIMD, with quadriplegia that prevented him walking and restricted the movement of his arms. He lacked verbal communication but was highly interactive with others and with a wide range of non-verbal and affective expression. His mother believed his understanding of verbal communication by others was good. He often showed awareness by anticipating events that were about to happen. Craig was about to become an uncle for the first time, and his mother wanted to develop a story to aid his understanding about babies and that the new baby was part of his family. His learning targets from school were to understand the difference between 'big' and 'small' and to reach out to explore objects, page by page, together with prompts and directions from the storyteller.

The story contains a number of references to baby Sophie and 'big' and 'small'. When the baby was born, Craig had his picture taken holding her and was able to give her a present. The school reported that from their perspective his learning targets had been met. This particular story is still very popular, so much so that *PAMIS* has had to produce a number of duplicates to meet demand.

The story of Lee

Five boys and three girls with PIMD, aged from 4 to 19 years, participated in the 'Sensitive Stories' project. The following vignette illustrates the learning potential and benefits for an individual, her or his family and the professionals involved.

Lee was an 11-year-old boy with PIMD and autistic spectrum disorders who had functioning hearing and vision. He communicated non-verbally, but could understand some verbal input. *Lee Goes to the Dentist* was designed to reduce his anxiety by familiarising him with the environment and the instruments involved, and to reduce teeth-clenching. The teacher used both speech and Makaton signs[1] in telling the story.

The significant pages depicted the dentist using three different instruments: a mirror, a toothbrush and a tooth polisher. These three significant pages occurred one after the other and encouraged Lee to open his mouth to use the instruments.

Behavioural analysis demonstrated that Lee engaged more with the story page in the final session relative to the first and median sessions, showing a characteristic reduction in looking at the storyteller. Touching the dental equipment objects and opening his mouth both increased. Lee's mother stated that the anxiety associated with opening his mouth and with the instruments had reduced, while his challenging behaviour reduced during storytelling. She reported that Lee associated the stimuli in the story with the instruments used at the dentist and he remained engaged with the story. She also stated that it had been a socially positive experience for Lee as he allows her to read the story to him at home, which had not been accepted with standard storybooks. Lee's teacher reported that Lee was focused during the story and used the objects more appropriately across sessions of storytelling. After two episodes of extreme aggression, Lee sat down to listen to his story.

Summary

In conclusion, research evidence argues for the effectiveness of multisensory storytelling in the areas of education, personal support and leisure. As research progresses, new questions are being raised that will lead to the further development of the approach. Multisensory storytelling for individuals with PIMD has already been extended to schools, with both individual and group work documented. The extension of the approach to one of the most challenging areas of PIMD, bereavement, is now being explored in the context of *PAMIS'* study of bereavement in people with PIMD and their carers.

Internationally, our hope now is that through joint efforts in research into and development of multisensory storytelling for people with PIMD, the approach will emerge as a well-validated method of addressing educational, therapeutic and leisure aims that complements other interventions in the lives of people with PIMD and their carers.

Try it yourself

Top tips

We have noted many of the key features of creating and delivering a multisensory story in the earlier sections of this chapter. Here are some of the key requirements to achieve these aims successfully:

- Ensure thorough preparation of the story, collaborating with the person with PIMD, family members and relevant professionals. Try out the materials and stimuli and then fine-tune them.
- The storyteller must prepare herself to present the story, learning the text to be spoken and the content of the cards. Practice presentation with a colleague so this is smooth.
- Remember you are telling a story. Make it active; use your voice to express what is happening in the story.

Where to go

Information on training and dissemination can be found on the **PAMIS** *website, along with a 4-minute video clip which illustrates the reality of multisensory storytelling.*

See the following websites for information about multisensory storytelling and its take-up by organisations:

- www.PAMIS.org.uk/_page.php?id=24
- www.docstoc.com/docs/73251109/Real-Lives-Real-Stories-The-Use-of-Multi-sensory-Storytelling (Documents for Small Businesses and Professionals)
- www.knowledge.scot.nhs.uk/home/search-results.aspx?q=%28string%28%22multi+sensory+stories%22%2c+mode%3d%22and%22%29%29&pm=fql&searchTerm1=multi+sensory+stories
- http://realisationandcommunication.wordpress.com/2011/03/15/palmis-multi-sensory-sensitive-stories/
- www.scotlandscolleges.ac.uk/curriculum/profound-and-complex-needs/profound-and-complex-needs.html
- http://teachinglearnerswithmultipleneeds.blogspot.com/2007/11/sensitive-stories.html (This US site disseminates resources and ideas for teachers of learners with severe, profound, intensive, significant, complex or multiple special needs)

Notes

1   Makaton signing is a system of key word signing to accompany speech. The signs are drawn from the sign language of the relevant country or culture, in this case British Sign Language. See www.makaton.org.

References

Brewer, J. & Hunter, A. (2006). *Foundations of multimethod research: Synthesizing styles*. London: Sage.

Evenhuis, H., Theunissen, M., Denkers, I., Versschuure, H. & Kemme, H. (2001). Prevalence of visual and hearing impairment in a Dutch institutionalized population with intellectual disability. *Journal of Intellectual Disability Research, 45*, 457–464.

Fenwick, M. (2005). Multisensory sensitive stories. *Eye Contact: RNIB, 42*, 12–14.

Fenwick, M. (2007). Sensitive Stories. *Insight: RNIB, 10*, 30–32.

Fuller, C. (1990). *Tactile stories: A do-it-yourself guide to making 6 tactile books*. London: Bag Books.

Fuller, C. (1999). Bag Books tactile stories. *The SLD Experience, 23*, 20–21.

Grove, N., Bunning, K., Porter, J. & Ollson, C. (1999). See what I mean: Interpreting the meaning of communication by people with severe and profound intellectual disabilities. *Journal of Applied Research in Intellectual Disability, 12*, 190–203.

Hogg, J. (2011). *What is the nature of people with profound intellectual and multiple disabilities? Philosophy and Research*. Presented at the First International Association for the Scientific Study of Intellectual Disability Asia-Pacific Regional Round Table on Profound Intellectual and Multiple Disabilities. Kyoto, Japan, 22 October 2011.

Hogg, J. & Sebba, J. (1986a). *Profound retardation and multiple impairments: Volume 1: Development and learning*. London: Croom Helm.

Hogg, J. & Sebba, J. (1986b). *Profound retardation and multiple impairments: Volume 2: Education and therapy*. London: Croom Helm.

Hogg, J., Juhlberg, K. & Lambe, L. (2007). Policy, service pathways and mortality: a 10-year longitudinal study of people with profound intellectual and multiple disabilities. *Journal of Intellectual Disability Research, 51*, 366–376.

Kittay, E. F. (2011). Forever small: The strange case of Ashley X. *Hypatia, 26*, 610–631.

Lambe, L. & Hogg, J. (2011). Multi-sensory storytelling: *PAMIS*' practice, experience and research findings. In B. Fornefeld (Ed.) *Multi-sensory storytelling: An idea gets through* (pp. 15–40). Berlin: Lit Verlag Dr. W. Hopf.

Maes, B. & Petry, K. (2006). Engagement and pleasure of children with profound multiple disabilities in interaction with adults during multi-sensory activities. *Journal of Applied Research in Intellectual Disabilities, 19*, 265.

Miller, J. (2003). Personal needs and independence. In P. Lacey. & C. Ouvrey (Eds), *People with profound and multiple learning disabilities: A collaborative approach to meeting their needs* (pp. 39–48). London: David Fulton.

Nakken, H. & Vlaskamp, C. (2002). Joining forces: Supporting individuals with profound multiple learning disabilities. *Tizard Learning Disability Review, 7*, 10–15.

Noldus, L. P. J. J., Trienes, R. J. H., Hendriksen, A. H. M., Jansen, H. & Jansen, R. G. (2000). The Observer Video-Pro: new software for the collection, management, and presentation of time-structured data from videotapes and digital media files. *Behavior Research Methods, Instruments and Computers, 32*, 197–206.

Penne, A. & Maes, B. (2011). Multisensory storytelling: Current research results. In B. Fornefeld (Ed.) *Multi-sensory storytelling: An idea gets through* (pp. 63–91). Berlin: Lit Verlag Dr. W. Hopf,.

Penne, A., ten Brug, A., Munde, V., van der Putten, A, Vlaskamp, C. & Maes, B. (2012). Staff interactive style during multisensory storytelling with persons with profound intellectual and multiple disabilities. *Journal of Intellectual Disability Research, 56*, 167–178.

Ross, E. & Oliver, C. (2003). Preliminary analysis of the psychometric properties of the Mood, Interest & Pleasure Questionnaire (MIPQ) for adults with severe and profound learning disabilities. *British Journal of Clinical Psychology, 42*, 81–93.

ten Brug, A., van der Putten, A., Penne, A., Maes, B. & Vlaskamp, C. (2012). Multi-sensory storytelling for persons with profound intellectual and multiple disabilities: An analysis of the development, content and application in practice. *Journal of Applied Research in Intellectual Disabilities, 25*, 350–359.

Vlaskamp, C., ten Brug, A. & van der Putten, A. (2011). Multi-sensory storytelling in the Netherlands. In B. Fornefeld (Ed.) *Multi-sensory storytelling: An idea gets through* (pp. 107–122). Berlin: Lit Verlag Dr. W. Hopf.

Watson, M., Lambe, L. & Hogg, J. (2002). *Real lives: Real stories.* Dundee: University of Dundee: *PAMIS.*

Young, H. B., Fenwick, M., Lambe, L. & Hogg, J. (2011). Multi-sensory storytelling as an aid to assisting people with profound intellectual disabilities to cope with sensitive issues: A multiple research methods analysis of engagement and outcomes. *European Journal of Special Needs Education, 26,* 127–142.

Young, H. B., Lambe, L., Fenwick, M. & Hogg, J. (2010). Using multi-sensory storytelling with people with PIMD. *Journal of Applied Research in Intellectual Disabilities, 23,* 497.

Chapter 12

Social Stories™

Carol Gray

Background

In an advertising campaign a few years ago, Starbucks encouraged us to 'Share your Story'; preferably, we can assume, over a cup of coffee! Marketing genius. People universally recognise, respect and respond to 'story' across country and culture. According to a research summary published in *Scientific American Mind*, we are 'wired' and naturally influenced by story, with links to our evolutionary history, as well as our social and emotional development, formation of beliefs and attitudes, and decision-making (Hsu, 2008). Story is the common thread of human culture and communication that, regardless of topic or purpose, supports us as we interpret, learn, share and organise our experiences.

It is unsurprising then, that when I introduced Social Stories™ as an instructional tool for use with children, adolescents and adults with autism spectrum disorders (ASD), parents and professionals immediately recognised an idea that 'just might work'. Just as 'story' plays an important role in human development and helps Starbucks persuade us to buy a cup of coffee, it also structures our efforts to teach social concepts and skills to those in our care. As we will explore in this chapter, Social Stories harness the positive potential of 'story' to support the social and emotional learning of individuals with ASD.

It could be said that Social Stories are patient and unassuming narratives of life on Earth. Each one shares accurate information with the audience, most frequently a child, adolescent or adult with ASD. As parents and/or professionals, you and I are the 'authors' who tailor the story to meet the needs of the audience. Each Social Story describes a situation, skill or concept according to procedures and a writing format defined by ten criteria. Addressing infinite topics, the criteria ensure an overall easy-going story quality, and a format, 'voice', and content that is descriptive and meaningful, and physically, socially and emotionally safe for the audience.

Principles

Social Stories are based on two signature principles. The first is a prerequisite acknowledgement that the *social impairment in autism is shared*. The definition of 'social' requires more than one person, rendering any 'social impairment' the responsibility of all who engage in a given interaction. The social challenge is equally rooted in mistakes on both sides of the social equation. Individuals with ASD are often unaware of the perspective of others and unable to interpret social context as fluently as their typical peers. This results in statements and behaviours that frequently take others, who regard the situation differently, by surprise. Parents, professionals, friends and family members may mistakenly attribute negative intent ('it's rude', '. . . impolite', '. . . offensive') to responses that seem quite logical to the person with ASD.

Closely related to the first principle, the second is to *abandon all assumptions*. Authors work from a non-judgmental vantage point as they research, write and implement each story. Concepts and terminology like 'inappropriate' have no value or purpose in the art and science of Social Story development. These terms reflect a social arrogance: 'my perception is the only right perception' that can derail even the very best of intentions. It is not surprising, then, that 'inappropriate' is one of seven forbidden terms that never appear in a Social Story.

These two principles form the foundation of all Social Stories. We gather information with a mind that is a 'clean slate', one that is minus judgment or preconception. The assumption-free vantage point is reflected in the selection of a Social Story topic, as well as its format, 'voice', text and illustration, and implementation. The recognition of a shared social challenge, along with a willingness to abandon assumptions that work so well for us most of the time, are the start-to-finish guiding principles of every Social Story.

History

I developed Social Stories early in 1991, while working as consultant to students with ASD at Jenison Public Schools, in Jenison, Michigan. I was working with one of my secondary students, Eric. Eric continually interrupted in class. Regardless of what his instructors said, Eric had a response. For years I had tried to teach Eric to raise his hand and wait for a turn to talk. Despite Eric's sincere and frequent promises to stop interrupting, his interrupting continued unabated. For all of our efforts, Eric had never – not once – independently raised his hand in class.

An all-school assembly marked a major turning point. The speaker walked onto the auditorium stage and said, 'I'm going to talk to you today about change.' Eric interrupted the assembly with an immediate response. The following day, I called Eric down to my office to review a videotape of the assembly. We took notes on a large display tablet as we compared our perceptions of what had occurred. Eric said there were two people in the assembly: Eric and the speaker. Suddenly Eric's 'interrupting' made sense to me. Eric was doing what I had taught him to do as a young child; if someone talks to you . . . answer. From Eric's perspective, he was being attentive and responding to each of his teachers.

After Eric had shared his description of the assembly it was my turn. Without discrediting Eric's ideas, I indicated that I saw about 500 students. In the course of comparing our notes, Eric said he wanted to stop interrupting. He began to create a 'to do' list. To my surprise, it was a list of all of the behaviours I had been trying to teach him. Upon his return to class, Eric's 'interrupting' was immediately replaced with a raised hand. Eric's success generalised to his other classes.

For years Eric had confidently told me that he would try to stop interrupting. I mistakenly assumed he knew what that *meant*. Despite my knowledge of Eric's social impairment, somewhere I was harbouring a mistaken attitude that Eric and I have the same set of social equipment. At the same time, I had underestimated his potential. Previous to the assembly conversation, if someone had asked me if Eric had the ability to apply an accurate description of an event to his own behaviour, I would have said no. Within a week of my conversation with Eric, I promised myself to abandon all assumptions when working on behalf of people with ASD.

Along with my instructional assistants, I began writing stories for students to share information that they may be missing. Success with one story led to writing another . . . and another . . . and another. A few stories were unsuccessful. Curious about those stories that had 'worked', we discovered that they all had a positive and supportive tone. We worked to identify and describe their shared characteristics (Gray & Garand, 1993). The article presented a research-based rationale and suggested the first guidelines for writing Social Stories.

The original guidelines have since been revised (Gray, 2004, 2010), updated, reorganised and expanded to emphasise safety and include the processes for research, development and implementation each Social Story (Gray, 2010). Referred to as Social Stories 10.1 (Gray, 2010) they are the most recent description of what is – and what is not – a Social Story.

Work in practice: Developing a Social Story

Initially, it may seem difficult to identify a Social Story that is 'typical' or representative. After all, most Social Stories are individually tailored for a child, adolescent or adult with a specific constellation of learning characteristics, interests and preferences. In addition, many story topics are untraditional, reflecting what may be singular perceptions, interpretations and conclusions of the audience. Despite these unique factors, each Social Story has the characteristic patient and positive tone (similar to the very first Social Stories) that renders it a suitable representative of the rest. In this section, I will briefly summarise the ten criteria that ensure Social Story quality.

The first two criteria get each new Social Story off to a good start. Authors begin with a goal to meaningfully and safely share accurate information with the audience (1st criterion: The Goal). A Social Story is often written in response to a challenging situation, to teach a new concept or skill, or to praise a current skill or achievement. Information is gathered from a variety of sources to help an author identify a specific topic (2nd criterion: Two-Part Discovery), and to set the stage for writing and illustration.

Most of the criteria structure story content and define the characteristics of the document. Consistent with sound story structure, each Social Story has a title, introduction and conclusion (3rd criterion: Three Parts and a Title). Information is meaningfully presented, with detailed consideration of the ability and learning profile of the audience (4th criterion: FOURmat). Additionally, audience interests are often included to make a story fun, interesting to review and potentially easier to recall and apply (9th criterion: Nine Makes it Mine).

The 5th criterion (Five Factors Impact Voice and Vocabulary) ensures the characteristic patient and positive tone of every Social Story. To maintain a non-judgmental tone, second-person statements never appear in a Social Story. Authors use first and/or third-person perspective sentences exclusively (1st factor). Information is presented positively (2nd factor). To support relevant connections between past, present and future, authors frequently include descriptions of related past experiences or possible future outcomes (3rd factor), often answering topical 'wh' questions in the process (6th criterion: Six Questions Guide Story Development). An individual with ASD may interpret statements literally. For this reason, vocabulary in a Social Story is carefully selected for accuracy (5th factor), and can be interpreted literally without changing the intended meaning of text and illustration (4th factor).

There are seven types of sentence in a Social Story (7th criterion: Seven Sentence Types). Descriptive sentences are required. Often called the heart of a Social Story, descriptive sentences factually describe the story context and main ideas. The other sentence types are optional and are used to describe the thoughts and feelings of others (perspective sentences); identify possible responses of the audience or those on his or her team (three sentences that coach); reinforce meaning of surrounding statements (affirmative sentences); or build interest and support comprehension (partial sentences).

To understand the role of the 8th criterion (A Gr-eight Formula), think back to the history of Social Stories and my conversation with Eric. Eric helped me to appreciate that he may not always be privy to the seemingly intuitive social information that guides most of us through each day. Providing accurate information helped Eric understand the rationale behind the behaviours that I was teaching him. For this reason, every Social Story describes more than directs. The 8th criterion defines the relationship between all of the sentence types to maximise description and minimise direction. It is central to the unassuming and respectful signature quality of every Social Story.

The 10th criterion structures the implementation of a Social Story (Ten Guides to Editing and Implementation). This equips authors with the information they need to edit, introduce and review a story, as well as check for comprehension and build related concepts and skills over time. It is the final checkpoint in the Social Story process, one that ensures that the positive patience of the document is reflected in the processes that surround it from start to finish.

The story of Andrew

Andrew is 9 years old and diagnosed with autism. His parents have an opportunity to go on a 3-week church choir tour of Germany. If they decide to go, it will mean that Andrew and his three sisters, Jennifer, Angela and Monica, will be staying with a series of church families. Considering the challenges that Andrew encounters with new situations, his parents decide to decline the invitation. The promise of a comprehensive Social Story reverses their decision. The story will provide Andrew with a one-page description of each day during his parents' absence.

Information is carefully gathered. Andrew's parents provide details regarding their schedule and that of their children. This information is merged with knowledge of Andrew's need for predictability and routine, and his cognitive strengths, reading abilities and illustration preferences.

The 21-page story is housed in a three-ring notebook that provides Andrew with a day-by-day description of his schedule, and that of his parents. The first page describes the events on the day of the tour departure, including visiting the airport and returning home with his first host family. The final page describes visiting the airport, picking up Mom and Dad, and returning home. To create a reassuring predictability, despite the different host families, each page in the body of the story shares a similar text and fill-in-the-blank format. For example, each page is titled, 'Andrew's Day on _____ (date)', followed by the same opening paragraph, sequencing (Andrew's day is described first, then that of his parents on the same day) and concluding statement. In advance of their departure, Andrew's parents interview each host family to complete the fill-in-the-blank statements. Each family is advised to select activities that are not likely to change or be cancelled to complete their page of the story:

Andrew's Day on _____.(date)

My name is Andrew. On this day _____ will take care of me. Most of the time we will be at _____ house. Jennifer, Angela and Monica will be there, too.

We will eat and sleep on this day. We will also do other things. We may

_____

_____

_____.

My mom and dad are in Germany on this day. They are singing for the people in Germany.

In _____ days, Mom and Dad will return. On that day, Mom, Dad, Sarah, Beth, Erica and I will return home.

Each page of the story includes a diary that Andrew may use to describe his day. Space is provided for photos or drawings. This makes Andrew an author of his own 'story'. At the close of the tour, Andrew will use his completed diary to tell his parents about his experiences during their absence.

To help Andrew keep track of the days remaining until his parents return, a simple calendar with 21 boxes is developed with a photo of each host family pasted on their corresponding date. At the conclusion of each day, after getting ready for bed and completing his diary page, Andrew places an 'X' through the day's box. Then he counts the remaining days. This number is inserted into the final paragraph of Andrew's story for the day; for example: 'In 8 days, Mom and Dad will return.'

Andrew's parents completed their tour, and Andrew completed his tour of host families with confidence. The story is credited with much of Andrew's success, as measured by Andrew's diary, the glowing reports from each host family and the relief of Andrew's mother, in particular.

Outcomes and evidence: What we look for

Social Stories are evaluated on two fronts. First, in practice, it is informal observation (like that of Andrew's parents) or basic data collection that often determines if a Social Story has 'worked'. For example, a mother writes a Social Story for her son, Zachary, about taking a bath. After one review of the story, Zachary's bath time tantrums disappear. Or a social worker develops a story for Angie, who never uses toilets outside her home. In the week following the introduction of the story, Angie uses the toilet at school ten times. Results like these earned initial credibility for Social Stories in the early 1990s, and have resulted in the enthusiastic affection of many parents, professionals and individuals with ASD that continues to this day

This grassroots acceptance of Social Stories preceded the second evaluation front of formal research. Social Stories have challenged scientific study (e.g. Reynhout & Carter, 2006). In practice, Social Stories are highly individualised, making them most suitable for case studies (Moore, 2004; O'Conner, 2009; Rowe, 1999). Case studies, however, provide little information about the value of Social Stories on a larger scale. In addition, Social Stories are frequently used in homes, classrooms, clinics and communities, where it is difficult to isolate variables that may impact results. Despite these challenges, and their relatively short history,

Social Stories are regarded as an evidence-based practice. In a major study to identify evidence-based practices and instructional interventions in the education of individuals with ASD, the National Autism Center (2009) listed 'story-based intervention packages' (with Social Stories identified as the most well known) as one of 11 established treatments for children on the autism spectrum, and Reynhout and Carter (2006) suggested that this was an intervention which was simple to implement and full of promise

Contexts of learning

Social Stories are likely to be most effective with students on the autism spectrum between the ages of 6 and14 years (National Autism Center, 2009, p. 50). Since their inception, it has been theorised that children with an early ability to read or interest in letters and numbers may be excellent Social Story candidates. However, I have on occasion developed simplified, straightforward, brief, home-based Social Stories (or elements of) for very young, preverbal children, with informally declared successes by their parents. Because they are stories with a supportive tone, it is suspected that Social Stories may be helpful for individuals with other learning challenges, or those without impairments. Research continues to help us to understand and more effectively harness the positive potential of Social Stories.

Cultural issues

As mentioned earlier, the goal of every Social Story is to share relevant social information. However, what may be relevant, valued and/or appropriate as a social skill in one culture may be undesirable in the next (see Meng, 2008). Cultures differ in the importance placed on the various and detailed aspects of many social traits, like independence and conformity. Additionally, even within a given culture, what is allowed or 'OK' in one family may not be acceptable practice in the home next door. To achieve the Social Story goal of sharing relevant information, the first step is to carefully gather information from a wide variety of sources. This always includes an individual's parents or caregivers. The required assumption-free vantage point supports not only the possible differences in social perception between audience and author, but cultural differences as well. It builds respect for cultural, social and familial norms (both expected and unforeseen) between author, audience and all others impacted by the story, into each story's foundation.

Try it yourself

We have learned a lot about Social Stories in their first 20 years as an instructional tool. Here are three important points:

Top tips

- Focus on process to achieve the best product. The processes used to develop and implement Social Stories are as important as the document itself. Take time to learn them, and use them consistently.
- Join others in protecting the integrity of Social Stories. We will be ever-increasing the availability of accurate information about Social Stories in the coming years. Stay continually curious about what is new with the approach. We look forward to hearing from you.

Where to go

Seek accurate information about the approach. The grassroots popularity of Social Stories has unfortunately given rise to a host of inaccurate and misleading websites. Start with reliable and accurate information, always available at www.thegraycenter.org and soon to be found also at www.CarolGraySocialStories.com. Worldwide training opportunities are always listed there. In addition, look for the Social Stories logo on training brochures and published materials, and seek workshops conducted by Team Social Stories and/or Social Story Satellite Schools and Services members.

References

Gray, C. (2004). Social Stories 10.0: The new defining criteria and guidelines. *Jenison Autism Journal*, *15*, 2–21.

Gray, C. (2010). Social Stories 10.1 tutorials. In *The new Social Story book: Revised and expanded 10th anniversary edition* (pp. xxv–lxxi). Arlington, TX: Future Horizons.

Gray, C. & Garand, J. D. (1993). Social Stories: Improving responses of students with autism with accurate social information. *Focus on Autistic Behavior*, *8*, 1–10.

Hsu, J. (2008). The secrets of storytelling: Why we love a good yarn. *Scientific American Mind Online*, 18 September. Available at: www.sciam.com/article.cfm?id=the-secrets-of-storytelling.

Meng, Hongdang (2008). Social script theory and cross-cultural communication. *Intercultural Communication Studies XVII: 1*, 132–138.

Moore, P. S. (2004). The use of social stories in a psychology service for children with learning disabilities: A case study of a sleep problem. *British Journal of Learning Disabilities*, *32*, 133–138.

National Autism Center (2009). *National standards report: The National Standards Project – Addressing the need for evidence-based guidelines for autism spectrum disorders*. Available at: http://www.nationalautismcenter.org/pdf/NAC%20Standards%20Report.pdf

O'Conner, E. (2009). The use of social story DVDs to reduce anxiety levels: A case study of a child with autism and learning disabilities. *Support for Learning*, *24(3)*, 133–136.

Reynhout, G. & Carter, M. (2006). Social Stories™ for children with disabilities. *Journal of Autism and Developmental Disorders*, *36*, 445–469.

Rowe, C. (1999). Do social stories benefit children diagnosed with autism in mainstream primary schools? *British Journal of Special Education*, *26*, 12–14.

Chapter 13

Storysharing™

Personal narratives for identity and community

Nicola Grove and Jane Harwood

Background

Storysharing™ is an approach based on researching and observing the ways we tell stories in everyday life. Within this framework, *narrative* is seen as the broad skill of recalling, sequencing and retelling an event – such as a factual account of the day, a scientific report, an explanation of why I am returning faulty goods or an evidence statement.

A *story* narrates a specific event which stands out from the everyday routine, and is meaningful enough for us to want to share the experience. We tell stories not just to provide information but to generate empathy and interest; we want listeners to share our reactions. We also want to make sense of our experiences, affirm who we are, relive an event in the imagination, give full rein to our creativity and to have fun. Above all, the form of the story imposes a pattern and a shape on the muddle of existence. Storysharing™ is distinguished by a collaborative approach: we tell stories *with* others, as well as *to* others. This approach is grounded in a social theory of narrative.

Theories

If you watch friends telling stories, or detach yourself enough from the process to observe yourself, you will notice some key aspects of oral, conversational telling that are very different from the stories you read on a page. The space is intimate – people lean in to each other. There is a rhythm to the telling and responding – narrator and audience perform a kind of dance that involves both voice (spoken words, sounds, exclamations) and movement, as the speaker gesticulates and listeners mirror, shifting body position in time with each other. If two people are telling there will be interruptions, switching, confirmations, challenges. The structure of the story is felt in the bones as the speaker uses pause, speed, pitch and intonation to build anticipation, reach a climax and wind down.

The rhythmic structure, emotional tension and release in the stories you tell as an adult are characteristic of the earliest exchanges with babies, as the work of Trevarthen (2005) and others shows (Fogel, 1992; Killick & Frude, 2010). So from the beginning, babies get a huge amount of practice in how to build up and resolve a tiny story.[1] Of course at first it is adults who structure the baby's experiences into these mini-tales. 'Oh no, did you fall down? Oh, poor baby. Naughty table, I'm going to give it a smack. There!' The next stage comes when the baby is able to signal a specific topic and pull it into the conversation. From birth, babies seem to be sensitive to the difference between new and old information (Roder et al., 2000). By their first birthday, children can attract attention to what is new and surprising – they will look and point whilst reacting and looking at the adult. This ability to attend simultaneously to an event and to another person is a critical stage in cognitive and linguistic development (Baker & Greenfield, 1988; Benigni et al. 1979). It is the beginning of true storytelling (Ellis, 2007).

Social constructionists see narrative as a social process, constructed with others over time. Fundamental theorists include Vygotsky (1978), whose term 'scaffolding' describes how adults provide structure which they gradually withdraw as the child becomes competent, Labov and Waletzky (1976), and Peterson and McCabe (McCabe & Peterson, 1991; Peterson & McCabe, 1983; Peterson et al., 1999). At first the child contributes maybe one piece of information – it is the adults who build the story (Scollon, 1979; Miller & Sperry, 1988), allowing children to experience what it is to be a competent and confident narrator, gradually taking more of a lead. Children appear to remember more detail of events if parents have engaged them in supportive, elaborated telling rather than focusing on the 'what happened', 'to whom', 'when' and 'where' (Bauer, 2007). Active, co-narrating listeners positively affect the way stories are told (Bavelas et al., 2000). Other important sources for the theory of Storysharing™ are Norrick (2000), who documented adult conversational stories, and Hymes (1981), whose work amongst First Nation peoples led him to emphasise the role of poetic structures in oral narrative speech. The principles are ones that we share with other programmes with an interactive focus (Forster, 2008, 2011; Forster & Iacono, 2010: *Hanging Out Programme*; Mosley & Tew, 1999: *Circle Time*; Nind & Hewett, 2006: *Intensive Interaction*).

Principles

The key principles are as follows:

- A story is built around an event that stands out as different enough to deserve our attention; Labov called this a 'reportable' event. Grey (2002) found that the earliest autobiographical memories in young children are built around atypical events.
- The event generates an emotional reaction (surprise, excitement, pride, amusement, fear, anger, sadness, curiosity, bewilderment), motivating us to share the memory.
- The event accrues meaning as we narrate it. Through telling we give a shape to the experience.
- The rhythm and musicality of the telling are as important as the content.
- Stories are told together, scaffolded by the more experienced partner.
- Questions are minimised to avoid the telling becoming an interview.
- The audience must actively listen and respond.
- Stories are repeated over and over again, for the enjoyment of seeing the audience react, and to shape the story further. This gives plenty of opportunity for it to become practised and internalised. The story may change over time but the core will always have the same elements and becomes relatively scripted.
- Care is taken not to overuse props, pictures and whiteboards, as these distract from the intimate dynamic of the telling space.
- Understanding develops gradually, through taking part in the story.

History

Storysharing™ developed out of the experience of running a storytelling group in a special school with a group of teenagers with moderate and severe learning disabilities, and later in work with adults and children with very profound disabilities.

I started with the intention of teaching children to retell a personal story individually. We would create an event (memorably, breaking an egg when trying to bake a cake) and then structure recall by immediately working in ones and twos using prompt questions: 'what happened first, next, then, finally, who did it, where we were' etc. Unfortunately, even with the help of symbol and picture cards, the children found it impossible to remember the story themselves. They could get one or two things right, but the task was too challenging. They also lacked the confidence to tell independently. In retrospect this was because they were all functioning below the age levels at which children are able to cope with these demands. Through trial and error we started telling the story as a group, so that the youngsters could join in as and when they wanted, linking events with the simple 'and then' rather than more complex constructions. This was successful, I think, because all pressure was removed and the model was continuously available – the children started by imitating, but over time contributed more of the narrative themselves. The approach was developed further through working in a day centre with around 20 adults, only two of whom had any functional speech.

Work in practice

A typical session lasts about an hour, including breaks and some group work. However, stories can be shared very quickly in short interactions, once people are familiar with the technique.

Who is here today?   Discovered perhaps with a song, marking the beginning of story time. This builds awareness of each other and allows everyone to become the focus of attention.

Who's got a story? What's happened?   Stories of the week, recorded by families or staff – something of significance to one or more people or to the community (class, school, home, town). A few illustrative props and a simple voice output communication aid[2] are used to support the participation of those who are non-verbal, shy or just love the recording device.

Create the space   A circle small enough for everyone to be heard and for a dynamic rhythm of telling and listening to build up, but not so close as to intimidate anyone.

Remind the group how to listen   Active listening involves joining in by saying something like 'Oh no!', 'Wow!', 'Really?', by mirroring gestures of the teller and by echoing key words.

Tell the story   The individual (maybe more than one) is encouraged with adult and peer support to join in telling. The structure of the dialogue involves:

- The invitation to listen: 'Guess what happened to Laura and Imram yesterday.'
- Sentences that the individual(s) complete, and reinforcement of these contributions.
- Encouragement to the audience to listen actively and empathetically.
- Closure or resolution, usually provided by the supporting adult.

In the following example, Laura and Imram are pupils. A basket of apples and a sticking plaster are props.

ADULT: We were in the . . .
LAURA AND IMRAM: Garden.
ADULT: Garden, yeah, and Laura was collecting the apples that had fallen down from the . . .

IMRAM: Tree.

ADULT: The tree, when suddenly Imram yelled, didn't you, you went . . .

IMRAM: Ow!

ADULT: And Laura dropped all her apples, didn't you, they all fell, they all fell . . .

LAURA: Down.

ADULT: And we rushed over to Imram and he was clutching his . . . (cues Imram by pointing to his knee)

IMRAM: Ow! (rubs knee)

LAURA: Knee.

ADULT: Because he'd tripped over a big branch and his knee was . . .

IMRAM: Bleeding.

ADULT: And Imram was so brave, he was amazing. It's OK now, though isn't it? Show everyone your knee Imram.

Everyone looks at and admires Imram's knee and responds with 'Wow!', 'Oh no!', 'Really brave'.

This story is likely to cue other memories of accidents (a fruitful source of anecdotes). So we ask if anything similar has happened to anyone else. There are many ways of developing the story:

- A permanent record, with a picture, object or scrap; for example, the bloodstained tissue, a photo of the apple, a piece of bark from the branch, and some words, written by the child or the teacher (see Musselwhite & Hanser, 2004). This is *not* a full literary exercise though you may choose later to develop a book or multimedia presentation.
- A drama, where children take turns to be Imram, Laura, the teacher, following Paley's (1991) inspirational guidelines.

It is critical to ensure that this is not the only time children tell the story. To become more independent narrators they need to tell it many, many times to new listeners – as we do ourselves.

We end the session with another song or ritual, thanking the tellers for their stories.

Assessment frameworks

We profile skills in six dimensions: *structural* (memory and sequencing for events); *feeling* (range of verbal and non-verbal emotions); *social* (getting and maintaining attention); *linguistic* (vocabulary, sentence construction); *poetic* (rhythm, narrative devices and figures of speech) and *active listening*. We also record the type of story and the balance between narrator contributions. This profile is used to identify strengths and needs in telling. It is applicable to fictional and imaginative as well as personal storytelling, and is culturally adaptable and dynamic (see Gutierrez-Clellen & Quinn, 1993).

For non-verbal individuals, we record levels of participation using the framework devised by Brown (1996):

Encounter	Learner is present during activity but shows no apparent awareness.
Awareness	Some awareness that something has happened.
Response	Shows response, begins to make distinctions.
Engagement	Attends and shows more consistent response to events.

Participation   Begins to take turns, anticipate and respond, with prompting.
Involvement   Spontaneously and actively joins in.

The stories of Ricky and Susie

Ricky and Susie took part in a Storysharing™ project that brought together children from special and mainstream schools in small groups.

Ricky was a very active 10-year-old with difficulties understanding, listening and relating to others. At first he was restless and rather disengaged, but once he became familiar with the structure he was an enthusiastic storyteller, and started to add information that made his stories very engaging. He learned to join in actively as a listener, responding to the stories of others. The final observations of Ricky were: 'He can remember the sequence of events, and use his voice and face to show lots of feeling. He loves the punchline: "Oh no, the doughnuts!" and adds a little coda of his own: "One yummy doughnut – and I ate it!"' He also connected with his mainstream partner – Ricky had felt sick on a sea crossing, and his friend said his sister had felt the same. Such tiny links are the building blocks of empathy. By the end of the project, Ricky was able to articulate feelings much more explicitly, saying to another child: 'You must be really said that your guinea pig died.'

Susie was a non-verbal 7-year-old with severe learning disabilities who also found it very hard to sit still and listen. Her mother was a wonderful support, making her stories each week in a picture book that she could join in retelling with props and a Big Mack.[3] Over time, she started to enjoy looking at the book, watching and listening as others responded to her experiences. She began to be a real group member, handing props to others when asked, and keeping very focused on her own story. Finally, she began to actively respond to the stories of others – when her partner told us about her visit to Diggerland, Susie leaned forward and looked at her. She smiled when she heard an 'Oh no!' response on the Big Mack, and she joined in with jigging up and down to represent how the digger moved.

Outcomes and evidence: What we look for

Evidence has been collected over a 10-year period from schools and residential and day services. Storysharing™ has been independently evaluated by Peacey (2010), who explored the impact of the approach on relationships between special and co-located schools, involving a total of 15 children with learning difficulties and 14 mainstream children (Grove et al., 2010). Between 2009 and 2011 the approach was used in residential settings with 12 adults with severe and profound disabilities, as part of a Mencap national programme to develop participation in decision-making (Involve Me[4]). We collected outcomes from a 3-year project in eight homes across Somerset, involving over 70 adults and 100 staff (Harwood, 2010). A new project is running in a special school from 2011 to 2014, with 50–60 children whose progress will be measured. In summary, the findings show that over the average 10-week period:

- Participation levels, expressive communication and listening increase in both frequency and range (i.e. the individual uses more vocabulary more often).
- Interactions between the individuals with disabilities increase.
- Staff become more confident as supporters, and use a wider range of strategies to elicit stories.

- As the archive of stories builds up, a real sense of community identity and friendship develops.

In our current project, young people are using personal stories to advocate for themselves in their leaver's review, families are creating stories for their children to share and staff are finding new ways of interacting. As one classroom assistant put it: 'We need to be behind the pupils, supporting them, rather than standing in front of them, asking questions and teaching them.'

Contexts of learning

Storysharing™ is designed to be maximally inclusive and is appropriate for pupils functioning at early developmental levels. Because it involves no pressure to communicate and lots of modelling, it can also be used with pupils who, for example, are struggling with a second language or who have social and emotional difficulties.

It is important to set aside enough time to share stories properly, so news time on a Monday morning is not ideal! However, you can use this session to identify what the good stories are. Within lesson times, English and personal social education or citizenship sessions offer good opportunities for Storysharing™. Small class assemblies at the end of the day or end of the week are ideal – the best stories can be told in school assemblies.

Stories can be used for empowerment in political contexts. Through Storysharing™, in 2011 a group of people with severe and profound disabilities in Frome told their stories to their member of parliament, persuading him to lobby against the planned removal of mobility benefit from disabled people in state-run homes.

Issues and limitations

With individuals on the autistic spectrum, telling personal stories presents challenges because, by definition, these involve an unpredictable or new event, associated with emotions, and requiring social interaction. With this group, and those who are anxious or overactive, we tend to downplay the unpredictable bits of the story and emphasise the ritualised elements. We start with what is known and feels comfortable, and gradually build up the story. We let them join in gradually, perhaps making brief contributions from the back of the room. For a similar graduated approach, see Peter & Sherratt-Smith (2001).

For those with complex health needs and a limited attention span it is important to keep the story very short and give them a role that plays to their strengths. For example, using rhythm and body movement with those who are deafblind. We have found that even if this person can contribute very little, the session often increases the awareness of others that here is a friend with a story, not just someone who sits passively in the room.

Ensure that supporting adults do not ask too many questions and do understand what makes a story. Routine information is hard to make interesting. Finally, the biggest challenge is getting stories from families. It can be hard for families to fit this in with all the other demands. At Valence School in Kent they have successfully used home–school books with a Big Mack, giving just enough information for the parent to get the gist of the story but leaving the punchline with the child. At Oakleigh School in London, Richard Barton, a parent support worker, has been running excellent groups with families from many different backgrounds, using picture prompt cards and working with memories and souvenirs of events (Barton, 2012).

Cultural issues

Personal storytelling is a very culturally specific activity. We know, for example, that Japanese, African American and Hispanic cultures tell anecdotes in ways that may differ from the expectations of white Western-educated teachers (see McCabe & Bliss, 2003). In brief, Japanese stories tend to be more concise, African American more elaborated and Hispanic to involve more orientation to family networks and relationships. The collaborative approach we describe here has been identified as standard in storytelling by children in some other cultures (Vernon Feagans et al., 2002; Scollon & Scollon, 1984). So it is really important to work with families to find out how and when they tell these little stories, what if any cultural constraints there are, and whether there are specific conventions they might use. Actually, this means that there are exciting opportunities to learn from the families and to involve them in the work you are doing.

Try it yourself

Top tips

- Spot the good stories as they happen in real life: capture them in your story butterfly net!
- Support and prompt, do not ask questions.
- Have a Big Mack ready and waiting!

Where to go

Openstorytellers and Nicola Grove run training courses and in-service training: www.open storytellers.org.uk.

Resources

- Forster, S. (2008). *HOP: Hanging Out Program: Interaction for people at risk of isolation.* Available to download from: www.cddh.monash.org/products-resources.html.
- Grove, N. (2010). *The big book of Storysharing*^{TM}*: At home, in school.* Available from SENJIT, Institute of Education, University of London or through www.openstory tellers.org.uk.
- Richard Barton can be contacted at: richardbarton@oakleigh.barnet.sch.uk for parent workshops.
- Technology we have found useful includes comic-book software for creating dynamic and fun records of stories, and story apps on the iPad that young people used in reviews and to share their stories with others. We used *Our Story* (see Appendix 2).

Acknowledgements

Openstorytellers gratefully acknowledge the support of the British Institute of Learning Disabilities; Somerset Partnership Board; the Community Team for Adults with Learning Disabilities in Somerset; the Esmee Fairbairn Foundation; the Paul Hamlyn Foundation and the Rayne Foundation. The contributions of these organisations have enabled the development of the Storysharing^{TM} programme.

Notes

1   An audio podcast of a lecture by Professor Trevarthen in 2009 demonstrates this very clearly: www.iriss.org.uk/resources/why-attachment-matters-sharing-meaning-colwyn-trevarthen [retrieved 16th March 2012].
2   www.communicationmatters.org.uk.
3   Big Mack is manufactured by AbleNet: www.ablenetinc.com.
4   http://openstorytellers.org.uk/pages/what_we_do.html.

References

Baker, N. & Greenfield, P. (1988). The development of new and old information in young children's early language. *Language Sciences, 10,* 3–34.

Barton, R. (2012). For the journey. SEN Magazine, 60.

Bavelas, J., Coates, L. & Johnson, T. (2000). Listeners as co-narrators. *Journal of Personality and Social Psychology, 79(6),* 941–952.

Bauer, P. (2007). *Remembering the times of our lives: Memory in infancy and beyond.* Mahwah, NJ,: Lawrence Erlbaum Associates.

Benigni, L., Bretherton, I., Camaioni,L. & Volterra, V. (1979). *The emergence of symbols: Communication and cognition in infancy.* New York: Academic Press.

Brown, E. (1996). *Religious education for all.* London: David Fulton.

Ellis, L. (2007). The narrative matrix and wordless narrations: A research note. *Augmentative and Alternative Communication, 23,*113–125.

Fogel, A., (1992). Movement and communication in human infancy: The social dynamics of development, *Human Movement Science, 11(4),* 387–423.

Forster, S. (2011). *Affect attunement in communicative interactions between adults with profound intellectual and multiple disabilities and support workers.* PhD dissertation: Monash University. Available at: http://arrow.monash.edu.au/vital/access/manager/Repository/monash:80098.

Forster, S. & Iacono, T. (2010). *Affect attunement between disability support workers and adults with profound intellectual disability.* Presented at ASSID 45th conference, 30 September 2010, Brisbane, Australia. Available at: http://www.asid.asn.au/Portals/0/Conferences/45thBrisbane/Conference %20Papers/Forster&Iacono_THU_1055_Communication61.pdf.

Grey, A. (2002). Children's earliest memories: A narrative study. *Australian Journal of Early Childhood, 27(4).* Available at: http://www.questia.com/googleScholar.qst?docId=5001505628 [accessed 13 March 2012].

Gutierrez-Clellen, V. & Quinn, R. (1993). Assessing narratives of children from diverse cultural/ linguistic groups. *Language, Speech and Hearing Services in Schools, 24,* 2–9.

Harwood, J. (2010). *Storysharing in Somerset 2008–2011: Final report.* Available at: http://openstory tellers.org.uk/pages/storysharing_final_report.pdf.

Hymes, D. (1981). *'In vain I tried to tell you' Essays in native ethnopoetics,* Philadelphia, PA: University of Pennsylvania.

Killick, S. & Frude, N. (2010). The teller, the tale and the told: the psychology of storytelling. *The Psychologist, 22(10),* 850–853.

Labov, W. & Waletzky, J. (1976). Narrative analysis: oral versions of personal experience. In J. Helm (Ed.), *Essays on the verbal and visual arts* (pp. 12–44). Seattle, WA: University of Washington Press.

McCabe, A. & Bliss, L. (2003). *Patterns of narrative discourse: a multicultural lifespan approach.* Boston: Pearson Education.

McCabe, A. & Peterson, C. (Eds.) (1991). *Developing narrative structure.* Hillsdale, NJ: Lawrence Erlbaum.

Miller, P. & Sperry, L. (1988). Early talk about the past: The origins of conversational stories of personal experience. *Journal of Child Language, 15,* 293–315.

Mosley, J. & Tew, M. (1999). *Quality circle time in the secondary school: A handbook of good practice.* London: David Fulton.

Musselwhite, C. & Hanser, G. (2004). *Creating and using remnant books for face-to-face communication and self-selected writing*. Chapel Hill, NC: Center for Literacy and Disability Studies. Available at: http://www.med.unc.edu/ahs/clds/files/how-to-handouts/RemnantBooks_000.pdf.

Nind, M. & Hewett, D. (2006). *Access to communication* (2nd ed.). London: David Fulton.

Norrick, N. (2000). *Conversational narrative in everyday talk*. Amsterdam: John Benjamins.

Paley, V.G. (1991). *The boy who would be a helicopter: Use of storytelling in the classroom*. Cambridge, MA: Harvard University Press.

Peacey, L. (2010). *A storytelling project in two sets of co-located mainstream and special schools in country and city: Findings from an action research project*. London: SENJIT Institute of Education.

Peter. M. & Sherratt-Smith, D. (2001). *Developing drama and play for children with autistic spectrum disorders*. London: David Fulton.

Peterson, C., Jesso, B. & McCabe, A. (1999). Encouraging narratives in preschoolers: an intervention study. *Journal of Child Language, 26,* 49–67.

Peterson, C. & McCabe, A. (1983). *Developmental psycholinguistics: Three ways of looking at a child's narrative*. New York: Plenum Press.

Roder, B., Bushnall, E. & Sackerville, A. (2000). Infants' preferences for familiarity and novelty during the course of visual processing. *Infancy, 1(4),* 491–507.

Scollon, R. (1979). A real early stage: An unzipped condensation of a dissertation on child language. In E. Ochs & B. Schieffelin (Eds.), *Developmental pragmatics* (pp. 215–228). New York: Academic Press.

Scollon, R. & Scollon, S. (1984). Cooking it up and boiling it down: Abstracts in Athabaskan children's story retellings. In D. Tannen (Ed.) *Coherence in spoken and written discourse* (pp. 173–197). Norwood, NJ: ABLEX Publishing.

Trevarthen, C. (2005). First things first: infants make good use of the sympathetic rhythm of imitation, without reason or language. *Journal of Child Psychotherapy, 31,* 91–113.

Vernon Feagans, L. S., Scheffner Hammer, C., Miccio, A. & Manlove, E. (2002). Early language and literacy skills in low income African American and Hispanic children. In S. Neumann & D. Dickinson (Eds), *Handbook of early literacy research* (pp.192–210). New York: Guilford Press.

Vygotsky, L. (1978). *Mind in society*. Cambridge, MA: Harvard University Press.

Chapter 14

Personal storytelling for children who use augmentative and alternative communication

Annalu Waller and Rolf Black

Background

Personal storytelling is a social activity vital to our day-to-day interactions. We tell others what we did, what we liked or did not like, how we laughed or cried. Telling stories involves turn-taking, naturally drifting from one story to the next with no knowing where you will end up. This makes it particularly challenging for augmented communication, where utterances must be prepared in advance.

Cheepen (1988) calls this type of talk 'interactional' conversation. She divides conversation into three main areas: speech-in-action, phatic communication and free narrative. Speech-in-action, or 'transactional interaction', refers to the goal-driven communication of needs and wants, and the sharing of information (Bowden & Beukelman, 1988). Phatic communication is used for social contact and etiquette – the 'glue' that keeps conversations going. Social closeness and the exchange and discussion of personal experiences, however, are best communicated through free narrative – or 'story'.

The term 'augmentative and alternative communication' (AAC) denotes strategies and systems that support the communication of individuals with little or no functional speech. People who use AAC tend to have a physical impairment and may have additional sensory and/or intellectual disabilities. Aided AAC systems range from the low-tech, such as symbol or word boards, to electronic devices such as single-switch voice recorders and high-tech voice output communication aids (VOCAs) with specialised software for spoken and written communication (Beukelman & Mirenda, 2005). Individuals also use unaided communication, including vocalisations, facial expressions and gestures or manual signs.

We know that the ability to relate and share personal experience is a complex skill that develops in early childhood, facilitated through scaffolding and successful experiential learning (Bruner, 1975). AAC devices support transactional communication well (Waller, 2006). They can be used for active participation in story retelling, through stored phrases or sentences, but AAC devices are not designed to support free narrative even though this accounts for the majority of conversation (Cheepen, 1988), making it difficult to scaffold personal storytelling with children who depend on AAC.

It is essential to support both *fictional* and *personal* storytelling through AAC. Unfortunately, in many cases it is only *fictional* storytelling that attracts attention in the classroom, within the context of literacy teaching. In this chapter we briefly discuss fictional storytelling. We then describe ways of supporting *personal* storytelling, using examples from the "How was school today . . .?" research project.[1]

AAC and fictional storytelling

Practitioners have developed innovative ways to involve children who use AAC in fictional storytelling. These strategies range from giving children the ability to choose what story they want to read at an early age, to supporting children to create their own stories. Light, Binger and Kelford Smith (1994) observed that when parents read bedtime stories to children with severe disabilities they were more likely to choose different books each time, unlike non-disabled toddlers, who chose their favourite stories over and over again. The Tango™ AAC device[2] includes phrases with which non-speaking children can prompt others to offer a choice of stories; for example: 'Ask me if I want a funny story or a scary story.'

Story vocabulary can be stored on AAC devices to allow children to participate in group storytelling; for example, a single word like 'boo!' on a single-switch device; key words such as 'bear' and 'Goldilocks'; phrases and sentences that allow interjections or links such as 'and then'.

Story writing is also supported within the classroom; learners are provided with templates and appropriate written vocabularies, with and without symbol support.[3] Learners are able to generate and tell simple stories by filling in different parts of the templates.

Engaging in fictional storytelling is important, but it is the sharing of personal experience which poses the greater challenge for children who use AAC.

AAC and personal storytelling

Challenges

Most children who use AAC access words and phrases by looking at and choosing pictures or words (a graphic interface). To find a word or sentence, the child needs to know the target item *and* remember where it is on the 'page'. There are three main strategies to help children locate a phrase or sentence: sequences of icon keys for a set number of core words (e.g. the Unity® system may use 'apple' + 'Action Man' to say 'eat'[4]); dynamic screens where the items are stored under a hierarchy of topic and activity screens (e.g. 'pets' 'places' 'days of the week' or 'chat' 'questions'[5]) and visual scene displays (items are accessed by pressing hotspots on a picture/photograph). Whatever the strategy, the child has to be proficient in knowing not only what words they want to access but where these are stored.

Whilst some children become skilled AAC users, their communication output is likely to be limited to one- or two-word utterances. Aided communication is characterised by the child responding to closed questions by a speaking partner. Successful storytelling is usually dependent on the conversation partner knowing the context of the story so that appropriate questions can be asked. A storytelling exchange which relies on information in a school-home diary might go:

MUM: I hear you went to the zoo?
CHILD: Might indicate 'yes' non-verbally.
MUM: And you saw a . . .?
CHILD: Penguin. (The parent may need to support the child to navigate through hierarchy of pages on the AAC device)

If the word 'penguin' was not on the device, the child might answer 'animal', prompting the parent to request descriptive information: 'What colour animal?' and 'Where does it live?'

As an alternative, school staff might store a structured story in the AAC device. Storytelling using this approach might result in:

MUM: I hear you've a story to tell. (Having read the home–school diary)
CHILD: My class went to the zoo today. We saw the penguins, the lion and the ostrich. (Parent may need to support child to navigate through hierarchy of pages to the 'story' page for today)

Strategies

The storytelling research projects at Dundee University[6] are developing systems and strategies to allow children to share their experiences in a conversational environment. Here we focus on the use of multi-message voice recording switches, such as the Step-by-Step[7] device, and high-tech symbol-based AAC devices based on touch-screen tablet computers.
Our aim is to:

* Enable children to relate their own experiences, including feelings and emotions.
* Promote interactive conversation in which all partners collaborate in the storytelling.
* Support multimodal communication, including vocalisations and non-verbal communication.
* Support children to communicate the meaning the story has to them – through providing ways of signalling feelings.

In order to achieve these aims, four stages must be completed:

1   **Story identification** The experience must be identified.
2   **Story preparation** The story vocabulary (content words and/or stored stories) must be stored in the AAC device.
3   **Story retrieval** The child needs to know what and where the vocabulary is stored.
4   **Story narration** The child needs to tell the story interactively.

Story identification

What is a good story? According to Grove (2010), an experience is worth telling if it has some meaning to the child. In natural conversations, stories emerge spontaneously. In the case of AAC, experiences with the potential to be a story must first be identified.
This task lies mainly with the person supporting the child at the time. Where possible, the child should be involved in identifying experiences of interest. This can be immediately after the experience or before a transition, such as returning to class from home economics or going home after school.

AFTER THE EXPERIENCE

Cameras are often used during the school day to capture photographs of important events, which can be used as prompts. A diary next to the child can be used to jot down interesting incidents. Both methods aid recall when preparing the AAC device and/or prompting/ scaffolding during subsequent narration.

BEFORE TRANSITIONS

Transitions provide powerful opportunities to share stories. In addition to the main transition of the day, going home, many happen during the school day, for example when a child returns to class after therapy. The aim is to empower the child to tell parents, siblings, fellow pupils and staff about what they have been doing.

Setting time aside with children before the transition to review the day or the recent activity is important to allow them to claim ownership of their stories. Reviewing the school day can be tricky if more than one staff member has been involved. Possible story events can be identified by: reviewing the child's timetable (did anything out of the ordinary happen?); messages or diary entries; using photographs taken during the day.

Story preparation

Having identified potential stories for the day, the next step is to prepare them for the AAC device. This can involve new voice recordings, inputting story texts or helping the child access existing or new vocabulary. For a successful interaction, the child needs to know how to access their story utterances before they tell the story.

When recording or storing new phrases, it is important to segment the story into separate utterances to ensure interactive telling – monologues make it difficult for a communication partner to interact with the child.

VOICE RECORDINGS

When preparing a device with new messages we employ the following strategies:

- Record all messages in the first person, as if the child were speaking.
- Record short messages with the minimum of information.
- Do not give all the information away in one message – build up the suspense.
- It is not always appropriate to include information the child can communicate without the AAC device (e.g. emotions), although this may be required to provide children with the experience of evaluation.
- It may be helpful to include empty messages at the beginning and end of a story. By recording a few seconds of silence for the first message we can avoid an unintended story start if the child hits the switch by accident. Silence or a definite story ending for the last message avoids a mistaken: 'Is that all?' question from a partner.
- If the device can store several stories (e.g. a high-tech device or multi-message recorder with different channels or levels) it is possible to retain favourite stories for longer-term use. In this case, beware of using time-restricted phrases like 'today'.
- Consider using an attention grabber function to help the child find listeners. For example, on some multi-message recorders a message can be repeated until a special button is pressed by the communication partner; on high-tech devices the child can repeatedly use a phrase.
- When using a high-tech device consider the child's physical abilities when deciding whether to store a story under one button (similar to a Step-by-Step) or several. Some children can be physically too exhausted after school to fully operate their high-tech device and it may be preferable to use a Step-by-Step to simplify access to the story.

Remember the main aim of personal storytelling. This is not about giving a *report* about personal experience. It is about enabling children to share and reflect on their experiences in a way that is entertaining for both themselves and the communication partner.

HIGH-TECH DEVICES

For high-tech AAC devices, story templates can be helpful. These provide a layout for the story messages, comments, access to related and older stories and utterances that support the interactivity (e.g. asking the communication partner about their experiences). Through research we have developed a story template for symbol-based dynamic screen devices (Reiter et al., in press; Black et al., 2010; Todman et al., 1995). This consists of four rows of five buttons in each row (see Figure 14.1 for a worked example).

Row 1: Operational functions (e.g. 'Close window')
Row 2: Story messages, beginning with a time reference (e.g. 'This was on Tuesday, 19th December')
Row 3: Perspective shift questions, allowing the storyteller to ask questions (e.g. 'Do you know Jenny?')
Row 4: Evaluation expressing emotions and judgement statements (e.g. 'That was good', 'I was scared') (see Labov & Waletzky, 1967)

Story retrieval

Stories emerge in social interaction. Hence the user must have ready access to the stories to tell them whenever the opportunity arises. This presents a challenge for several reasons:

• Multi-message devices usually only have the ability to save a maximum of three stories at any one time – stories are recorded over each other and then deleted.
• The child needs to have ready access to the device. If you have to take the Step-by-Step out of the bag before you can tell the story, the moment is gone. Instead, place the device so it is ready to use at all times (e.g. on a lap tray) or use devices that can easily be carried around by children who can walk.
• If a device can store several stories, make sure the most appropriate story is readily available.
• High-tech devices usually have one story button/page reserved for the story of the day. This should be available on the home page so the child (or support person) does not have to search for it.
• If multiple stories are stored the user needs to be able to find them. This seems relatively easy with a small number of stories but as the number of stories increases, retrieval becomes more difficult. Make sure that stories are stored under easily remembered codes/dynamic displays.

It is imperative that children have the opportunity to retain (and collect) their favourite stories. Telling and retelling stories is an essential part of language development. The only way to keep stories using current multi-message devices is to transcribe the recordings before stories are over-recorded, a strategy employed by the Bridge School in San Francisco (Hamilton, 2010). In order to support more effective multi-message storytelling, research at Dundee (Reiter et al., in press) is developing a mobile phone multi-message application that allows for the recording of many stories. In the meantime, important stories need to be made available on multi-message recorders (i.e. re-recorded) to allow learners to relate experience from the past.

Retaining stories is simpler on high-tech AAC devices, where a story page can have several buttons relating to different stories (e.g. *The Horseriding Competition* or *My 10th Birthday with the Magician*). Each story button links to the appropriate page based on a template. However, the child still has to remember where the story is stored; current devices make it very difficult for users to find stories by keywords (e.g. inputting 'magician' or 'horseriding').

Story narration

Narrating a story is an interactive process. By storing stories in short segments the user is able to step through the story, inviting comments and questions from the conversational partner (see Peter's story below). Figure 14.1 illustrates how segments can be stored to facilitate turn-taking. The child is also able to add evaluations to the story – these are not built into the messages, but can be used to reflect the child's emotional response to the event as the story unfolds.

This story page in Figure 14.2 was created to support the story of pupils being snowed-in at school. The second row is used for the story utterances:

CALENDAR: This was in December 2010.
SNOW: We had so much snow. The school was really struggling.
BUS: There was even so much snow that the buses would come to pick us up!
CAMP: I and some of my friends had to stay at the school overnight!
PIZZA: The teachers drove to ASDA to get medicine and a pizza.

The question-mark buttons allow the narrator to ask about the partner's respective experiences: 'Did you have much snow?', 'Were you ever stuck somewhere?' The bottom row is reserved for generic evaluations, such as positive/negative phrases: 'It was great', 'It was bad' and story-specific evaluations: 'It was a bit scary'. Additional buttons are provided for yes/no responses. A 'next' button was introduced to allow the telling of the story step by step.

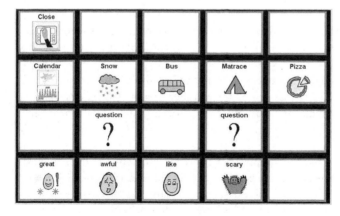

Figure 14.1 A story page on a symbol-based dynamic screen device.

The story of Peter

10-year-old Peter has athetoid cerebral palsy, with very little functional speech. He has difficulties accessing technology, using a combination of gross and fine motor movements for switch access or eye pointing with an E-Tran[8] folder. His multi-message device is mounted on the lap tray on his wheelchair.

During a therapy session, Peter played a new card game, 'pairs', with Sarah, his therapist. Each player uncovered pairs; Peter using eye pointing. The game was a great success. However, after collecting almost all the card pairs, one single card was left – a cat was missing its partner.

Sarah encouraged Peter to tell his class about his success, as they had not known whether or not he would master the game. She suggested each message to Peter before recording it onto the device. The following message sequence was designed to raise the conversational partner's curiosity and prompt questions which would be answered by the subsequent interaction.

1   I played my new pairs game with Sarah.
2   I won the game 4–3.
3   The cat was missing.
4   Where's the cat?

Message 1 sets the scene and prompts the question 'And who won?', hence the second message. However, message 3 introduces a twist in the tale. The most interesting part of the experience was the missing card – this led to plenty of excited interaction during the game: 'Where was it? Did it get lost? Where was it hiding?' So a fourth message was added to reflect this fact. Peter replayed the messages before returning to class. Both authors were in the session and everyone enjoyed reliving the experience as Sarah prepared Peter's story with him.

As everyone walked back together to class, Peter enthusiastically pressed his switch, going through the story. When he met his teaching assistant in the corridor, the story had advanced to its last message: 'Where is the cat?', 'I know where the cat is!' she exclaimed as she turned around to fetch it from the classroom. A lively discussion about the story ensued with much hilarity.

Evidence

Studies in which children were given the ability to relate past experience interactively suggest that children are able to take more control in a conversation if they have access to personal stories (Black et al., 2010; Waller et al., 2001). They are able to initiate and respond better to questions. They also show increased self-esteem (Waller, 2006; Waller et al., 2001) and development of storytelling skills (Waller & O'Mara, 2003).

Try it yourself

Try to identify an activity which has resulted in some emotional response – laughter/frustration/success. Record a story onto a multi-message recorder or high-tech device. Send the child to visit another class or teacher to tell their story.

Top tips

- Identify interesting stories during the school day: what do the speaking children talk about, what is interesting to the child?
- Practice is everything – important for both the child (to access the story) and the supporting person (for recording it).
- Create opportunities (big and small) for the child to tell their story in school – weekend news on Monday morning with stories from home; coming back to class from therapy, swimming, playtime, after lunch etc.

Where to go

- For further information about the project, visit http://aac.computing.dundee.ac.uk.
- For information on AAC, visit www.communicationmatters.org.uk and www.isaac-online.org.

Notes

1   See www.computing.dundee.ac.uk/projects/howwasschooltoday [retrieved 19 February 2012].
2   See www.dynavoxtech.com/products/tango [retrieved 19 February 2012].
3   For examples of story templates with symbol support, see literacy materials from www.donjohnston.com/products [retrieved 19 February 2012] and www.widgit.com/resources [retrieved 19 February 2012].
4   See www.prentrom.com/unity [downloaded 23 February 2010] for an example of a sequence-based retrieval system.
5   See for example CALLTalk by CALL Scotland: www.callscotland.org.uk/Home.
6   See http://aac.computing.dundee.ac.uk [retrieved 19 February 2012].
7   See www.ablenetinc.com/Assistive-Technology/Communication/BIG-LITTLE-Step-by-Step™-with-Levels [retrieved 19 February 2012].
8   The E-Tran (eye-transfer) folder contains pages of communication items (symbols and pictures). Each page of items is organised in blocks. Each block has a colour frame, as does each symbol/picture. To select an item, the child first selects the page by indicating 'yes' when the target page is reached. The child selects the block that contains the target item by looking at the colour on a colour bar; the item is then chosen by looking at the colour surrounding the actual item.

References

Beukelman, D.R., & Mirenda, P. (2005). *Augmentative and alternative communication: Supporting children and adults with complex communication needs.* London: Paul H. Brookes.

Black, R., Reddington, J., Reiter, E., Tintarev, N. & Waller, A. (2010). Using NLG and sensors to support personal narrative for children with complex communication needs. *Proceedings of the NAACL HLT 2010 Workshop on Speech and Language Processing for Assistive Technologies* (pp. 1–9). Los Angeles, USA, 1–6 June. Stroudsburg, PA: The Association for Computational Linguistics.

Bowden, P. & Beukelman, D. (1988). Rate, accuracy, and message flexibility: Case studies in communication augmentation strategies. In L. Bernstein (Ed.), *The vocally impaired* (pp. 295–311). Philadelphia, PA: Grune & Sutton.

Bruner, J. (1975). From communication to language: A psychological perspective. *Cognition, 3,* 255–289.

Cheepen, C. (1988). *The predictability of informal conversation.* Oxford: Printer Publishers.

Grove, N. (2010). *The big book of storysharing.* London: SENJIT, Institute of Education, University of London.

Hamilton, H. (2010). Read all about it! 'Home News' informs AAC System development and instruction. *Proceedings of the 14th Biennial Conference of the International Society for Augmentative and Alternative Communication.* Barcelona, Spain, 24–29 July. ISBN: 978 0 9684186 9 7.

Labov, W. & Waletzky, J. (1967). In J. Helm (Ed.), *'Narrative analysis'. Essays on the verbal and visual arts* (pp. 12–44). Seattle, WA: University of Washington Press. Reprinted in *Journal of Narrative and Life History* 1997; 7: 3–38.

Light, J., Binger, C. & Kelford Smith, A. (1994). Story reading interactions between preschoolers who use AAC and their mothers. *Augmentative and Alternative Communication, 10,* 255–268.

Reiter, E., Tintarev, N., Waller, A. & Black, R. (in press). Natural language generation for augmented and assistive technologies. In A. Stent & S. Bangalore (Eds.), *Natural language generation in interactive systems* (Chapter 2). Cambridge: Cambridge University Press.

Todman, J., Elder, L. & Alm, N. (1995). Evaluation of the content of computer-aided conversations. *Augmentative and Alternative Communication, 11,* 229–234.

Waller, A. (2006). Communication access to conversational narrative. *Topics in Language Disorders, 26,* 221–239.

Waller, A. & O'Mara, D. (2003). Aided communication and the development of personal story telling. In S. von Tetzchner & N. Grove (Eds.), *Augmentative and alternative communication: Developmental issues* (Chapter 11, pp. 256–271). London: Whurr.

Waller, A., O'Mara, D., Tait, L., Booth, L. & Brophy-Arnott, B. (2001). Using written stories to support the use of narrative in conversational interactions: Case study. *Augmentative and Alternative Communication, 17,* 221–232.

Chapter 15

Describing and evaluating the storytelling experience

A conceptual framework

Tuula Pulli

This chapter describes an approach to multisensory storytelling developed in Finland with children and adults with severe disabilities, using a model which emphasises aesthetic, social and cognitive aspects of a drama-based interaction that goes beyond speech and provides novel ways to cope with the limits of human capacity.

Background

Traditional narratives such as epics, legends, fairy tales, poems and songs tell us who we are and how we cope with the social and the natural world. Their images and archaic characters arise from an eternal shared past and future. This property belongs to everyone. It can and should be accessible to everyone, and explored irrespective of physical or mental skills. The best stories succeed in moving us because they are based on the origin of human mind and body, beyond all formal languages. (Grove, 2005; Peter, 1994, 1995, 1996; Ricoeur,1991; Turner, 1982, 1995). Multisensory and co-experienced storytelling with a rich range of artistic experiences refreshes our minds and enhances shared attention to a common interest for children and adults who have difficulties in perception, social life, cognition and speech. It provides not only an access to culture but also a way of implementing community-based rehabilitation (Grove & Park, 1996, 2001; Maes et al., 2007; Mitchell & van der Gaag, 2002; Peter, 2003; Pulli, 2010.)

Work in practice

Traditional narratives can be told with severely disabled persons in various ways. There are three main approaches, which can also be combined:

Performance   One or more storytellers perform a story using rich body language (such as voice variations, space and rhythm). Additional multisensory items (such as fire, music, dance, choir, sound effect, blowing air or smell) or a few objects (such as food, mask on face, clothes or blanket) may be also used. The aim is to intensify the feeling of presence by providing concrete clues that convey the worlds which exist behind the story themes and metaphors we are using.

Co-creating   The storyteller acts as a 'conductor' to organise participation by the audience, providing material for them to use. For example, for making fire they may wave sparkles or colourful silk scarves. In exploring characters they may wear cloaks, hats or make sounds. They may remain seated or, voluntarily yet guided, move across the room or step on stage for a short moment. The conductor or the performers group is in charge of the action.

Adapted process drama   The group tells the story together and explores chosen themes. They follow freely the pre-text made by the conductor(s), who also take responsibility for conveying the gist of the plot and prompt the group to perform episodes. Participants can reflect spontaneously on what has been told, what is happening or will happen, why it happens or what else might happen. They may act as a choir or take on roles. Support workers can be grouped or paired with the persons with disabilities – sharing participation and roles with them. When co-creating interaction in episodes seems to flow, the conductor(s) reduce their guidance. They remain responsible, however, for story clarity and dramatic tension, and group dynamics and psychic safety. For working ethically, they use various conventions in drama education (e.g. O'Toole, 1992, 1996).

All approaches are enriched by artworks such as music, colour and movement, which may be created together or picked up. In *Odyssey Now*, projections of images from relevant art galleries are used as illustrations (Grove & Park, 1996; see also Carroll, 2000).

Sharing an experience: Staff members cross between worlds

More capable persons support the less capable ones but they simultaneously experience the event as participants. For the staff too, a fictive, magical and substitute world offers a haven to throw oneself into. Research documents accounts by support workers: they describe having found novel ways of interaction that do not take place in daily routines. They also report having noticed positive, unused capacity, which hides behind challenging or withdrawing behaviour (Dobson et al., 2002; Maguire, 2003; Pulli, 2010). A lived experience endures, and enriches everyone (Conroy, 2009; van Manen, 1990). While experiencing the magic together we emerge as members of the group. For many, belonging to a group or a performance is more important than communication, as Ferguson (1994) says: "We sit in the boat of Odysseus and float on a stormy ancient sea [*we wave; the wheelchairs surrounded by dark blue silk on our skin*]. Suddenly we get wet [*because someone sprays us with water*]. Fellows, take the rope!"

An intensified shared story moment brings us emotionally close and makes us sensitive to each other. This breaks down the barriers between ability and disability, and points to equality. In a story world we can look from a distance but still explore things close up and through our bodies. Thus we may justify Heidegger's (1927) observation that as a being everyone is anyone.

Assessment and planning frameworks

Grove (2005) has developed a framework that allows teachers and therapists to explore and analyse the responses of pupils to rich imaginative experiences in ways that help them plan and evaluate their sessions. The motivation for this was in fact the remarks of a sceptical bureaucrat in the government-run curriculum authority, who poured scorn on her hesitant suggestion that assessments should be designed to take into account responses such as the spontaneous, fleeting but magical eye contact made by a very autistic teenager during an episode of *Macbeth* (Grove & Park, 2001). The ideas for the framework came from the world of arts education (Ross, 1978; Webb, 1992), special education (Brown, 1996) and cultural theory (Geertz, 1973). The dimensions considered are: *engagement* (using Brown's model, which moves from *encounter* – being present – to active *involvement*), *feeling* (empathy and affect), *cognitive* (thinking and language) and *aesthetic* (creativity, social impact, formal properties). Figure 15.1 provides a schematic outline of the approach (for full details see Grove, 2005). Fornefeld (see Chapter 10) and McCaffrey (see Chapter 3) have also developed multidimensional frameworks that take account of creativity, emotional responses and aesthetic properties.

The framework devised in the course of my own research on storytelling by adapted process drama with severely disabled and speechless adults (Pulli, 2010) drew on some of these ideas. The conceptual framework is based on the links between special education, drama and art education, speech and language therapy, and critical education philosophy. These four disciplines are approached by phenomenology and hermeneutics, focusing embodied knowledge (see Dillon, 1991; Kolb, 1984; Merleau-Ponty, 1970, 2002; van Manen, 1990). Content analysis has demonstrated that those disciplines and approaches share the ethics of concern for otherness, communality, equality, empowerment, alternative ways of viewing, creativity, knowledge in action and experiential learning. Similar ideology can be found in the literature of devised and applied drama (e.g. Baldwin, 2008; Hellier-Ticono, 2005; Nicholson, 2005a, 2005b). I explored the conceptual model in analysing the responses of 18 disabled participants and 16 staff members (12 videotaped sessions, each 60–90 minutes, time range 6 months). The framework was useful in describing, under-standing and evaluating the emergence of themes and other rehabilitative items, and what was happening during and after sessions.

There are three dimensions in the model shown in Table 15.1: *aesthetic* (beauty/ lived experience), *social* (sharing/ partnership) and *cognitive* (comprehension/ understanding).

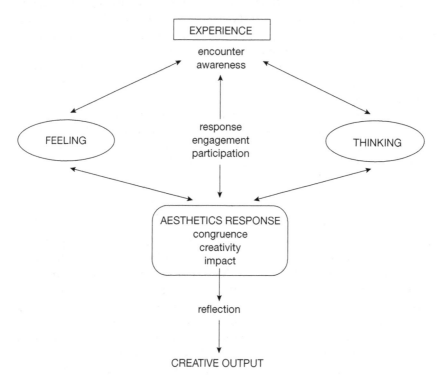

Figure 15.1 Response to literature: an evaluative framework.

Table 15.1 A framework for developing narrative skills through multisensory storytelling

	Dimensions		
	Aesthetic	Social	Cognitive
Art education			
Why?	Art *itself,* as a *value*	Art as a shared *process*	Art as a means of *experimental learning*
Dimensions in storytelling	*Beauty*	*Partnership*	*Comprehension*
What?	Performance form: space, rhythm, tension Sensation Appraisal Flow	Membership Equality Co-creating	Forming images Seeking insight Meaning-making Symbol function
The experience of storytelling	*Lived experience*	*Involvement*	*Understanding*
How?	Apprehension Embodied knowledge Feeling	Inner/outer activity Mutual respect Turn-taking	Wondering Viewing in other ways

Beauty   refers to responding to the artistic form by sensation, appraisal and feelings evoked by the story – a lived experience arises in an immediate and unconscious apprehension which stays in the memory of embodied knowledge.

Partnership   refers to involvement and sharing which arise in the process of living the story through together, as an equal member of the group – audience and actors are all participants.

Comprehension   refers to learning about the world by forming images and meanings, and by exploring different options – it arises in wondering what and why something is told in the story and how it connects to real life (see Carroll, 2000; Nicholson, 2005a, 2005b).

Guidelines for implementing and evaluating multisensory storytelling

The aesthetic dimension: Use the principle of beauty to design story presentations in order to create lived experience

Some principles of the following guidelines are common in applied drama (e.g. Baldwin, 2008; Hellier-Ticono, 2005; Nicholson, 2005a, 2005b). They have long been a focus in early interaction methods (e.g. Coupe & Goldbart, 1978; Nind & Hewett, 1994).

Frame a session with plain structure – like a picture frame, which separates the image from the background, unobtrusively. Use 'initial hooks': everyday materials in new settings, such as snow or the smell of a horse in a living room. Use opening and closing rituals. Make transitions slowly. Wait – repeat – ritualise – surprise – rest – reflect, over and over again. Increase tension gradually but decrease it fast and early.

Create impressions of shifting in space and time (use a mask, a light, an odd sound, a frozen movement, a sound effect). Provide aesthetic experiences by distinction and contrasts (such as noise before silence, light before darkness) but do not exaggerate stimulation (see Grove & Park, 1996 on concepts of foregrounding and backgrounding in multisensory environments).

While liberating oneself from the past and the future you and the participants may achieve full presence and flow.

Assess and evaluate the lived experience noticing how the participants:

Focus on a story   Pause in expectation, use their senses, seem to be present.

Move through an imaginative world   Play seriously, leave routine behaviours behind, accept dramatic tension.

Throw themselves into   Follow and/or play 'make-believe', step into a pretend world knowing that it is not real.

The social dimension: To create a shared feel of 'us', a community, make it clear that partnership arises only in respect and love

Support everyone to feel that they are equal and unique. Take care of individual territories and allow voluntary participation. Everyone – the staff included – has the right to determine the degree to which they join in. Never force, correct or instruct: 'do it this way'. Repeat and ritualise: 'we all do this', enticing them to join a magic circle of shared beliefs and meanings.

For co-creating, suppress your own ideas when you become aware of an idea or initiative made by a participant. If a passive person demonstrates any activity (voice, gesture etc.) which could be interpreted as carrying a meaning in the actual episode, respond to it positively. Encourage others to reinforce it as well.

Help the participants to feel how the characters feel and what they want. In our voyage, it is not only the captain who faces a challenge, we all do. Structure the story so that people at all levels of ability are enabled to take part. In early interaction skills, the goal of joint attention may be sufficient – to focus on the same target (light, sound etc.) with the partner or group. In Grove and Park's *Macbeth* resource (Grove & Park, 2001), which is structured to promote social cognition, joint attention is the foundation of all of the activities.

Within the social dimension, evaluate how the participants:

Become empowered   Influence the action, sense being important to others; for example by sitting in the middle, calling out.

Show membership   Aim for a common goal, seek and get help, seem to feel empathy.

Interact with each other   Reflect, initiate, respond, take turn, cooperate; for example joining in clapping, giving a rope to a fallen sailor.

The cognitive dimension: To develop comprehension, let people learn by wondering and by doing

Provide problems with options and new horizons, but also things that they already know and can do. Choose one, two or three themes and make them visible; clarify but do not explain. If you are using a process drama approach, stick to the plot but allow for changes and breaks, and make the participants feel that by mutual respect almost anything is allowed to happen.

Use real objects, pictures, gestures, signs and any other forms of communication to substitute for and support speech. However, do not stick to any particular language form and do not expect all to understand the plot. Each creates his own meanings: one person may try to establish causes and effects, another may recognise familiar objects, a third may think on a character's feelings or goals. Simplify archetypes (well-known characters such as Cinderella or the witch) by marking them with one item (e.g. bare foot, wooden spoon) and characteristic behaviour (e.g. witchy laugh, sweeping the floor). Do not use theatre spectacle but a miniature stage. Symbols and meanings arise in a story without the same chaos of time and space where they exist in everyday life.

Create anticipation using intensified attention. For instance, a trumpet sound is heard but nothing else happens – yet. Someone may learn to expect the sound to be repeated. Another may learn to expect a king's appearance. Someone may even try to guess the king's thoughts. Let these different levels shift and intertwine. In storytelling, as in real life, we manage quite well in guessing – using love, respect and good will.

Within the cognitive dimension evaluate how the participants:

Form mental images   Assign meanings to objects and actions; learn marks or symbols referring to something that is not necessarily present.

Wonder   Contemplation through looking for a long time, smiling, repeated touching; seek connections and explanations – asking 'what/to whom/why this happens'.

Try to find new points of view   Seek new solutions, encounter different persons and gain insight to them.

Why the crown of a king in a story is attractive: Three ways of answering the question

Baroque music is playing and a golden crown is slowly passed around a circle. All sit calmly, waiting for their turn to hold the crown to play the role of king. Then something surprising takes place. While wearing the crown an autistic youngster who normally finds it hard to sit still waves his hand, first imitating his caregiver. He then continues on his own to act like a king. He looks at the audience and raises his hands like a king to greet the people, and interacts with them non-verbally. He then sits down calmly and takes a deep breath. How could this happen, when he does not seem to consciously know what a crown, king or power means?

- An *aesthetic* explanation lies with sensation, apprehension, and emotion. A shiny, distinctive object, combined with aristocratic music, stimulated him to accept the offered gesture.
- A *social* explanation relies on the desire to get attention and acceptance from the group. They shared a common goal. He noticed that the others wanted to have the crown, and so did he. He desired to be part of a shared and empowering experience.
- According to a *cognitive* explanation he had an inner clue that the crown may possess a meaning, is something more than an interesting object. Without knowing history he realised that a crown may change not only person's looks but also his image. He explored this idea – the idea of a symbolic function – by curiosity leading to knowledge. He seemed to have capacity to learn to read and use symbols, perhaps also for learning a language. He may also have memories of this behaviour from television, books or theatre – the important thing is that he is drawing in these memories and using them appropriately.

Summary

Persons with special needs have the right to learn about the cultural heritage of stories that give rise to questions about life and ourselves – that move everybody. The best stories do it in concrete and abstract ways simultaneously, and these can be combined in hands-on work. Thus classic literature can provide basic experiences performed with aesthetic sensation (*beauty*), with respect and love (*partnership*) and with clarity of meaning (*understanding*). These three dimensions form an evaluation model for multisensory storytelling in education and community-based rehabilitation. Stories can be performed by storyteller(s), co-created with an audience, or told by adapting process drama with all persons who are present. In all approaches, the participants' embodied knowledge interfaces with symbolic interpretations in a story – for the *equal* and the *eternal* to emerge.

Resources

- www.art-stream.org (creates artistic opportunities for individuals in communities traditionally under-served by the arts)
- www.avoin.jyu.fi/draamakasvatus (a Finnish centre delivering drama education at Jyväskylä University)
- www.idea-org.net (International Drama/Theatre and Education Association)
- www.fideafinland.fi (Finnish Drama/Theatre Education Association)

Acknowledgement

Thanks to Nicola Grove, who was one of the four supervisors in the research. She found the framework internationally interesting and adaptive. Her products and enthusiasm influenced the text. *Odyssey Now*, especially should be kept alive – it is an eternal book of archetypes and a storytelling manual beyond cultures.

References

Baldwin, P. (2008). *The primary drama handbook*. Thousand Oaks, CA: Sage.
Brown, E. (1996). *Religious education for all*. London: David Fulton.
Carroll, N. (2000) (Ed.). *Theories of art today*. Madison, WI: University of Wisconsin Press.
Conroy, C. (2009). Disability: Creative tensions between drama, theatre and disability arts. *Research in Drama Education: The Journal of Applied Theatre and Performance, 14(1)*, 1–14.
Coupe, J. & Goldbart, J. (1978). *Communication before speech*. London: Croom Helm.
Dillon, M.C. (1991). Merleau-Ponty and postmodernity. Foreword in M.C. Dillon (Ed.), *Merleau-Ponty Vivant* (pp. ix–xxxv). New York: State University of New York Press.
Dobson, S., Upadhyana, S. & Stanley, B. (2002). Using an interdisciplinary approach to training to develop the quality of communication with adults with profound learning disabilities. *International Journal of Language and Communication Disorders, 37*, 41–57.
Ferguson, D. (1994). Is communication really the point? Some thoughts on interventions on membership. *Mental Retardation, 32*, 7–18.
Geertz, C. (1973). *The interpretation of cultures: Selected essays* (pp. 3–30). New York: Basic Books.
Grove, N. (2005). *Ways into literature: Stories, plays and poems for pupils with SEN*. London: David Fulton.
Grove, N. & Park, K. (1996). *Odyssey Now*. London: Jessica Kingsley.
Grove, N. & Park, K. (2001). *Social cognition through drama and literature for people with learning disabilities: Macbeth in mind*. London: Jessica Kingsley.

Heidegger, M. (1927). *Sein und Zeit*. Tübingen: Max Niemeyer Verlag.

Hellier-Ticono, R. (2005). Becoming-in-the-world-with-others: Inter-act theatre workshop. *Research in Drama Education, 10(2)*, 159–173.

Kolb, D. (1984). *Experiential learning: Experience as a source of learning and development*. Englewood Cliffs, NJ: Prentice Hall.

Maes, B., Lambrechts, G., Hostyn, I. & Petry, K. (2007). Quality-enhancing interventions for people with profound intellectual and multiple disabilities: A review of the empirical research literature. *Journal of Intellectual and Developmental Disability, 32(3)*, 163–178.

Maguire, N. (2003). Group counseling for people with mild to moderate mental retardation and developmental disabilities: an interactive-behavioral model and a single session. Video review, ed. by V. Brabender. *International Journal of Group Psychotherapy, 53(1)*, 125–128.

Merleau-Ponty, M. (1970) Trans. 1963. *In praise of philosophy and other essays*. Evanston, IL: Northwestern University Press.

Merleau-Ponty, M. (2002). Trans. 1962, rev.1981. *Phenomenology of perception*. London: Routledge & Kegan.

Mitchell, J. R. & van der Gaag, A. (2002). Through the eye of the cyclops: Evaluating the multi-sensory intervention programme for people with complex disabilities. *British Journal of Learning Disabilities, 30*, 159–165.

Nicholson, H. (2005a). *Applied drama: The gift of theatre*. New York: Palgrave.

Nicholson, H. (2005b). On ethics. *Research in Drama Education, 10(2)*, 119–125.

Nind, M. & Hewett, D. (1994). *Access to communication: Developing the basis of communication with people with severe learning difficulties through intensive interaction*. London: David Fulton.

O'Toole, J. (1992). *The process of drama: Negotiating art and meaning*. London & New York: Routledge.

O'Toole, J. (1996). Towards a poetics of drama research. In P. Taylor (Ed.), *Researching drama and arts education: paradigm and possibilities* (pp. 147–155). London: Falmer Press.

Peter, M. (1994). *Drama for all*. London: David Fulton.

Peter, M. (1995). *Making drama special: Developing drama practice to meet special educational needs*. London: David Fulton.

Peter, M. (1996). *Art for all*. London: David Fulton.

Peter, M. (2003). Drama, narrative and early learning. *British Journal of Special Education 30*, 21–27.

Pulli, T. (2010). *Totta ja unta* [The real and the illusory]. Drama as a means of community-based rehabilitation and experience for persons with severe learning and speech disabilities. Doctoral dissertation in special education: Jyväskylä University: Studies in Education, Psychology and Social Research. (Summary in English, 7 pages).

Ricoeur, P. (1991). Life in quest of narrative. In D. Wood (Ed.), *On Paul Ricoeur: Narrative and interpretation* (pp. 20–33). London: Routledge.

Ross, M. (1978). *The creative arts*. London: Heinemann Education.

Turner, F. (1995). *The culture of hope: A new birth of classical spirit*. New York: Free Press.

Turner, V. (1982). *From ritual to theatre: The human seriousness of play*. New York: Performing Arts Journal Publications.

Van Manen, M. (1990). *Researching lived experience: Human science for an action sensitive pedagogy*. New York: State University of New York.

Webb, E. (1992). *Literature in education. Encounter and experience*. London: Palmer Press.

Resources

Organisations

There are societies for storytellers and storytelling all over the world. Here we list main sites for the UK and Ireland.

Society for Storytelling
Morgan Library
Aston Street
Wem, SY4 5AU
Tel.: +44 (0)7534 578386
Web: www.sfs.org.uk

The Society for Storytelling offers events, a magazine and a website. The society welcomes anyone with an interest in oral storytelling, whether teller, listener, beginner or professional. There are subgroups to cater for specialist interests such as storytelling in education or therapy. You can find storytellers by searching their directory, and there is a list of festivals and events where you can take people to hear stories. By joining the society you get many benefits, including a weekly update of events and access to news groups.

Scottish Storytelling Centre
43–45 High Street
Edinburgh, EH1 1SR
Tel.: +44 (0)131 556 9579
Web: www.scottishstorytellingcentre.co.uk

Supports a national network of storytellers involved in outreach projects with local authorities, environmental agencies, community centres and libraries, engaging with all age groups and diverse cultures of modern Scotland and providing opportunities for the socially and educationally excluded to take part in community-based, inclusive cultural experiences.

George Ewart Evans Centre for Storytelling
Cardiff School of Creative and Cultural Industries
ATRiuM
University of Glamorgan
Adam Street
Cardiff, CF24 2XF
Tel.: +44 (0)1443 668631
Web: http://storytelling.research.glam.ac.uk

Based at the University of Glamorgan, the centre is dedicated to promoting, teaching, developing and researching storytelling in all its forms. It runs courses and conferences.

The Story Museum
Rochester House
42 Pembroke Street
Oxford, OX1 1BP
Web: www.storymuseum.org.uk

Centre for children's literature and storytelling.

Verbal Arts Centre
Stable Lane and Mall Wall
Bishop Street Within
Derry/Londonderry
Northern Ireland, BT48 6PU
Tel.: +44 (0)28 7126 6946
Web: http://www.verbalartscentre.co.uk

Based in Derry, Northern Ireland, this is a centre which promotes the verbal arts, with a strong educational programme.

Storytellers of Ireland
Web: www.storytellersofireland.org

Aims to promote the practice, study and knowledge of oral storytelling in Ireland through the preservation and perpetuation of traditional storytelling and the development of storytelling as a contemporary art.

Sign language and deaf storytellers
http://www.learnbsl.org/Learn_British_Sign_Language_-_Stories_in_the_Air_-_BSL_Dictionary_learn_online/About_Stories_in_the_Air.html

Story collections

www.timsheppard.co.uk – One of the most informative sites, with collections of stories, information on national and international storytellers and organisations, festivals and courses.
www.livingmyths.com
www.mythstories.com – A web-based museum of myth and fable.
www.healingstory.org – For stories to address health and difficult situations.
www.story-lovers.com
www.storynet.org
www.openstorytellers.org.uk – This community group, which uses both personal and traditional stories to develop social inclusion, is setting up an archive of traditional stories relating to the experience of disability.

Digital storytelling

Technology

Use of emerging mobile technologies and electronic communication is increasing in social environments and interactions, and recently within teaching and learning practices.

The field is moving so fast that it is inevitable that anything we list here in terms of specific applications is likely to be out of date soon after publication. The applications listed here relate to personal storytelling, as there are literally hundreds of programmes and apps dedicated to imaginative stories and book-making.

The iPhone, iPod and iPad are revolutionary aids to storytelling as they are portable, relatively cheap and, perhaps most importantly, carry status and enable those with special needs and disabilities to use the same devices as everyone else. At the time of print, they are the best resourced and most reliable platform for applications but there are others emerging with different application resources, such as Android. Digital first-person video narrative can be created with users by combining recorded voice, still and moving images, and music or other meaningful sounds. They can often act as a medium that can increase engagement and motivation for hard-to-reach users and so can be the trigger for improving independent communication and participation.

In relation to the face-to-face dynamic storytelling which is the focus of this book, it is important to bear in mind that technology can be a support for oral telling, through the provision of illustrations, or an alternative way to tell – for example, a very autistic person or a person with profound disabilities may find it much easier to create and share a digital story than an oral or signed story. What the applications do is provide creative and fun ways of recording and sharing stories, and ways of developing recall and structuring of content.

A feature of technology that makes resources such as applications so useful is the flexibility that can be achieved to quickly and immediately change and update stories through the use of photos of real-life people/places/objects/events that can be easily adapted for story expansion or development. This is not the case with hard copy versions of stories.

At the time of publication there were three main applications for personal storytelling, using uploaded photos and images, that were popular in special schools:

Scene & Heard a way of animating an image or video and creating a narrative with symbol support.
www.therapy-box.co.uk/scene_and_heard.aspx
www.widgit.com/products/third_party/scene_and_heard/index.htm

Our Story has been designed by a team at the Open University as an aid to storytelling and literacy for young children and those with special educational needs. It is a free app.
http://itunes.apple.com/gb/app/our-story/id436758256?mt=8
Information about the background and theory for the app can be found at: http://creet.open.ac.uk/projects/our-story

Stories About Me has been specially designed for individuals with autism. This site also has a very helpful overview of the evidence base for the use of iPad apps in the field of special needs.
www.limitedcue.com/our-apps/

Because applications are continually changing and developing, it is worth trying to find out about the possibilities for content adaptation by reading user reviews when you preview applications. It is worth double-checking whether an application is designed for use on an iPad and/or an iPod/iPod touch as there can be variation in features available.

Reviews

An excellent presentation on storytelling apps of many different kinds, by Shelly Terrall, can be viewed at: http://www.slideshare.net/ShellTerrell/jalt-2011-kids-sharing-stories

Inov8 is an organisation which provides reviews of useful technology for special needs. A review of storytelling apps can be found at: http://www.inov8-ed.com/2012/05/theres-a-special-app-for-that-part-11-creative-apps-for-digital-storytelling/

Other reviews are readily available by typing in relevant key words.

Thanks to Rachel Keen, Specialist Speech and Language Therapist, Kent Communication and Assistive Technology Service, for her advice on technology.

Index